DATE DUE

A Neal-Schuman Special Report

A Practical Guide to Internet Filters

Karen G. Schneider

NEAL-SCHUMAN NETGUIDE SERIES

NEAL-SCHUMAN PUBLISHERS, INC.
NEW YORK   LONDON

Published by Neal Schuman Publishers, Inc.
100 Varick St.
New York, NY 10013

Printed and bound in the United States of America

ISBN 1–55570–322–4

Table of Contents

Acknowledgements

It took a village to write this book: vendors, librarians, friends, library staff; my family, Sandy, Emma, and Dot; Bob Messina, my project officer at the Environmental Protection Agency, who encouraged me to keep "timeclock hours" so I could get this project done; the Reverend Tracey Lind, who understood why I played hooky from church every Sunday for six months; and my patient editor, Charles Harmon.

THANKS TO VENDORS

The vendors who worked with me went far beyond the call of duty. Many vendors took the time to ask me what I thought libraries wanted, and were open-minded enough to engage in philosophical discussions about privatized information, the validity of blocking data, and other topics I wish our library community would be able to discuss so openly.

My particular thanks to Bob Stahr and Kevin Fink of Bess; Susan Getgood of Cyber Patrol; Joe Field and Judy Hogaboom of Cyber Snoop; Dan Sydow and Travis Priest of I-Gear; Patrick Fischer of Smart Filter; Andy Campbell and Mark Weaver of The Library Channel; Susan Larson and Alexandra Salomon of Surfwatch; and Tom Stansell and Kevin O'Brien of Websense. Thanks also to the Recreational Software Advisory Council for allowing me to reprint their Web rating system.

THANKS TO THE FOLKS IN THE TRENCHES...

Particularly the contributors to the chapter, "Advice from the Trenches": Frank Bridge of Austin Public Library; Hank Long of Englewood Public Library, Colorado; Judy Teachworth, Jean Tabor and Wendy Woltjer of Canton Public Library, Michigan; David Burt of Lake Oswego Public Library, Oregon; Lisa Champelli and Chris Jackson of Monroe County Public Library, Indiana; Eloise May of Arapahoe Library District, Colorado; James LaRue of the Central Colorado Library System; Karen Hyman of the South Jersey Regional Library Cooperative; Duncan McCoy of the Boulder City Public Library; and Myron Estelle of the Cumberland County Library, New Jersey.

IN GRATITUDE TO THE TIFAP TEAM

I cannot say "thank you" in any way that expresses the extent of my gratitude toward the volunteers in TIFAP, The Internet Filter Assessment Project, which has its own chapter in this book. These librarians gave extensively of their personal time, their talents, and their computers (which were sometimes mangled by the products they tested). Theirs was a hugely generous gesture to the library community, and role-modeled a paradigm shift, if I may be so trite, in how librarians approach new products. We all owe a huge thanks to the librarians who gave so much personal time to evaluating filters. The following are the volunteers who submitted information; a few more were quiet well-wishers and observers—the crowd cheering us on.

TIFAP HALL OF FAME

Though I didn't recruit from any particular pool, the TIFAP volunteers overwhelmingly have experience in reference and public-access services, about half are manager/supervisors, and several have migrated to the "techy" environment of library systems maintenance.

Susan Barb is an Adult Services Librarian at Orange Public Library, Orange, California. Susan, who tested Surfwatch in Phase 2, participated in TIFAP "to get firsthand knowledge of how filters operate. This will enable me to educate my library board regarding their pros and cons before decisions are made."

Marie Bryan is the Library Services Director at Woodland Public Library, California. Marie tested Cybersitter in Phase 2 and Net Nanny in Phase 3. Marie said, "participation in this project allows me to develop local policy from a position of knowledge."

Frank Cervone is the Assistant Director for Systems at DePaul University Libraries, Chicago, Illinois. Frank became involved in TIFAP to gain "some actual experience using some of these tools." Frank tested Bess in Phase 2.

Jennifer Cram is the Manager of Library Services, Queensland Department of Education, Brisbane, Australia. Jennifer participated in TIFAP because "we need facts, not hype!" She helped develop and test questions in an unfiltered environment.

Heidi Cramer is a public-service Librarian at Newark Public Library, New Jersey. Heidi tested Cyber Snoop for Phase 2. Heidi participated in TIFAP as a "learning experience" so she could be a resource for her colleagues.

Thomas Dowling wrote the script for the Phase 2 and Phase 3 surveys and provided other technical advice. He's a bit shy, but it's believed he has some kind of technical position in the Midwest.

Sheryl Dwinell is a Database Management Librarian and Cataloger at Marquette University Libraries, Milwaukee, Wisconsin. Sheryl tested Cybersitter for TIFAP Phase 2 and provided invaluable feedback on the original survey design. Sheryl became involved in TIFAP because she is concerned about "the implementation of filtering software in libraries before there has been detailed analysis and testing by librarians...I'm involved out of a concern for freedom of information."

Myron Estelle is a LAN Adminstrator and Reference Department Head at Cumberland County Library in Bridgeton, New Jersey. Myron tested Smart Filter in Phase 3. He has independently evaluated several of the products TIFAP looked at, and participated in TIFAP "to get a perspective on the subject from other librarians involved with the subject area, to lend my year's worth of experiences to others, and to learn of possible alternative theories and methodologies."

Rich Gause is a librarian on the Eastern seaboard who tested Websense in Phase 2 and Phase 3. Rich believes that "we (librarians) shouldn't make ill-informed decisions and I shouldn't leave it up to others to do the work."

Dianne Harmon is an Associate Director at Joliet Public Library, Illinois. Dianne and her son Kevin helped test questions in an unfiltered environment. Dianne believes that "public libraries need to be proactive rather than reactive over patron concerns over the Internet."

Amy Helfman is a Public Services Librarian at Hebrew Union College, New York, New York. Amy tested questions using Yahooligans, Yahoo's website for children. Amy believes that "it's important that librarians keep their prerogative to select materials, even on the Internet...I am concerned about balancing the need to make sound judgements against the need to avoid censorship."

Karen Hyman is the Executive Director of the South Jersey Regional Library Cooperative in Gibbsboro, New Jersey. Karen tested Cyber Patrol in Phase 2, Phase 3, and with the "Lite" settings. Karen participated in this project to "contribute to a factual information base on filtering products."

Hal Kirkwood is an Assistant Manager and Economics Librarian at Purdue University, West Lafayette, Indiana. Hal , who helped develop test questions and the surveys, is participating in TIFAP out of an "interest in the topic and fear of a loss of control to commercial vendors." Hal stresses his "belief in the First Amendment and personal/parental responsibility" when it comes to information on the Internet.

Jerry Kuntz is an Electronic Resources Consultant for the Ramapo Catskill Library System in Middletown, New York. Jerry tested Net Nanny for Phase 2 and I-Gear for Phase 3, and is the developer and maintainer of a filter-vendor survey that was a key source of information for TIFAP. Jerry became involved in TIFAP because of his interest in "possible technical solutions to concerns about acceptable use," and thinks that "an ideal solution would be a filter that can be selectively applied by patrons or...parents/guardians."

Nettie Lagace is Coordinator of User Services, The Internet Public Library, Ann Arbor, Michigan. Nettie participated in TIFAP "because libraries can't abdicate the selection of information in this great new medium to commercial parties." Nettie added that participating in TIFAP was "energizing." Nettie tested Cyber Patrol in Phase 3.

Carole Leita is a teacher, web manager and consultant with the Infopeople project in Berkeley, California. Carole, who has a Masters in Library Science, tested Cyber Patrol in Phase 2 and Phase 3. She wants to "help to provide those using filters...a usable filter, and if not possible, provide testimony as to why."

Paul Neff is a Technology Services Manager at Arlington Heights Memorial Library in Illinois. Paul also has a Masters in Library Science. Paul provided assistance with the survey question design for

Phases 2 and 3. Paul participated in TIFAP "to be better informed, and to better inform others about the capabilities of filtering technology."

Vicki Nesting is a Branch Head at New Orleans Public Library, Louisiana. Vicki tested Surfwatch in Phase 2 and Smart Filter in Phase 3, and provided extensive feedback on the distribution schemes for the test questions. Vicki says that "curiosity" spurred her initial involvement in TIFAP, and added that she has concerns about legal liability of libraries using filtering software.

Susan Oliver is a Principal Librarian at the Tampa-Hillsborough Public Library in Tampa, Florida. Susan tested Cyber Patrol in Phase 2 and with the "Lite" settings. Susan says she is "interested in how we provide electronic information to our customers and how we teach them to best use it on their own...I feel that I will be better able to discuss the issues and come up with ideas if I am more familiar with some of the alternatives."

Jill Patterson is a Senior Librarian at Glendora Public Library, California. Jill is involved in TIFAP out of "personal and professional interest." She is a Cyber Patrol tester. Jill feels that "filters are only partially effective" and she wants "to see a comprehensive, comparative survey."

George Porter is a librarian at Cal-Tech. He tested Bess for Phase 2 and Phase 3, and came up with the pronunciation for TIFAP.

Keely Price is a Reference Librarian at Lewiston Public Library, Lewiston, Maine. Keely tested Cyber Snoop in Phase 2. Keely was interested in TIFAP because filtering is "a hot topic in librarianship" and "since it is feasible that I could one day work in a library that wants to use filters."

Rivkah Sass is a Research Engineer at Thomson Technology (and has a Masters in Library Science). Rivkah helped develop test questions. Rivkah believes that it is "the role of parents to determine what their children see and use on the Internet." Rivkah is particularly interested in PICS.

Lisa Shackelford is the Manager of the Village Library in Oklahoma City, Oklahoma. Lisa tested Bess and The Library Channel for Phase 2 and Phase 3, and provided invaluable editorial assistance with question design and question distribution. Lisa says, "I've listened to enough debates on this topic, where no one had any clear data to back up their arguments. I decided that I'd rather help than wait to see what others found out."

Leila Shapiro is a Regional Librarian at Bethesda Regional Library, Maryland. Leila helped develop the original test questions. Leila says she participated in TIFAP because "it is important that libraries know everything about filters just as they learn everything about the other resources they purchase." Regarding filters in libraries, Leila said "I believe it is wrong to purchase unknowns."

Saralyn Shone is a Computer Systems Specialist at Arlington Public Library, Texas. Saralyn tested Cyber Patrol for Phase 2 and Phase 3. Saralyn participated in TIFAP because she wants "to be able to evaluate different projects and help make the best decision to meet our unique community needs."

Bo Simons is an Internet Librarian at the Sonoma County Public Library, California. Bo wants to learn "the nuts and bolts of filters to help increase the fund of knowledge" in this area. Bo tested The Library Channel for Phase 2 and Phase 3.

Nancy Turner is a Systems Librarian at Thomas Branigan Memorial Library in Las Cruces, New Mexico. Nancy tested Net Nanny for Phase 2 and Phase 3. Nancy participated in TIFAP "as a way of educating myself about using the Internet for reference and what the pros and cons of filters will be when our library goes public with providing Internet access...I will also have better knowledge of 'what is out there' and how 'easy' it is to get at it."

Harry Willem is a consultant and assistant director of the Southeast Kansas Library System. Harry tested Netshepherd in Phase 2, and has personally looked at several other products. Harry is interested in "accurate testing and results" regarding the use of Internet filters in library settings.

Introduction

Librarians everywhere are struggling with what is easily the most difficult issue our profession has ever faced: whether Internet content can or should be limited in library settings. This has generated megabytes of discussion, most of it more emotional heat than helpful light.

A Practical Guide to Internet Filters attempts to discuss Internet content filters as tools with performance issues. Though I have my opinions, which I discuss later in this chapter, I am not "pro" or "anti" filter any more than I am "pro" or "anti" automobile. The annual *Consumer Reports* car issue does not include a debate about whether cars are good or bad; this book's approach is similar. Here are our needs; here are the tools; here are the shortfalls. What you do with this information is your decision. Use it to select a filter; use it to decide not to use a filter; use it to study the issue some more; refute the entire book with your own efforts.

WHAT THIS BOOK OFFERS

In *A Practical Guide to Internet Filters*, I first walk you through descriptions of different filtering methods and the software tools used to filter. The chapter on planning your purchase includes schedules, sample signs, and guidelines for evaluating products prior to purchase. After this, I offer some perspectives on filtering from librarians who have decided whether or not they will filter, and apply my thoughts to web rating systems such as PICS, the Platform for Internet Content Selection.

I begin the section on production evaluations by talking about a six-month project, TIFAP (The Internet Filter Assessment Project), in which librarians evaluated filters in real life—how filters perform, what they do and don't do, and how librarians respond to a variety of Internet content. The original questions we used to test filters are included in the appendix. I wrap up with product reviews.

NOT ALL FILTERS ARE DISCUSSED

The product discussions focus almost exclusively on products evaluated in TIFAP. Other products exist; others will crop up. However, for the near future, the features described in this book apply to all known products. Vendors will always claim that their product is the unique, exceptional software that circumvents the problems other products have. Hold the product against the criteria in this book, evalute the product in a working information environment, and decide for yourself.

WHEN THE INFORMATION CHANGES . . .

This book has a website:

   http://www.bluehighways.com/filters/

As information becomes available, I will provide updated data on each product or new feature (though you will have to refer to the book to make complete sense of it).

BACKGROUND ON THE EMERGENCE OF FILTERS

For most of us, the Internet has become an indispensable medium for all kinds of information. The Internet's many freely-available government, educational, not-for-profit, commercial, and self-published resources have expanded library services for even the smallest libraries in ways that even five years ago most of us would not have anticipated. Additionally, the technology on which the Internet is based has proved to be a viable backbone for offering commercial databases and the contents of online catalogs. Librarians have discovered that their users want, and need, Internet services. Offer a class on using your catalog, and a few information die-hards show up; offer a class on the Internet, and you will not have enough seats for everyone who shows up. The Internet is not going away, and the rapid appearance of electronic versions of many traditional paper-based resources suggests that books already have competition from other quarters.

What makes the Internet wonderful is also the source of its greatest controversy. The good, the bad, the ugly, the inaccurate, and the outdated: the Internet democratically brings all of it to our living rooms, schools, and libraries. With the click of a mouse, we can read about new air pollution standards, follow the burial of Princess Diana, learn opposing viewpoints on abortion, play chess, buy books, send money to a favorite cause, make acquaintances, and view child pornography. In no other medium except, perhaps, a New York subway do we see so many examples of human strengths and frailties jostling side by side.

THE INTERNET AS CULTURE CLASH

The Internet doesn't fit any model we know. In traditional collection-development, we carefully select books, CD-ROMs, and other databases in our libraries from catalogs and other resources that themselves represent a level of culling; few, if any, major library vendors offer self-published books, instructions on bomb-making, or pornography.

Some librarians say that money is the only obstacle to owning these many other resources. Yet if all resources were equally desirable, wouldn't they show up in libraries in equal quantities? We do make decisions about resources we intentionally purchase; with these selections, we are not only acting *in loco parentis*, but *in loco community*.

I am not suggesting that the presence of resources we wouldn't select means we should block them. Some librarians believe strongly that libraries should consider the Internet an opportunity to provide all available information, and that intentionally limiting information is a form of censorship. I *am* suggesting that the Internet is completely different from any other information medium we have experience with, and our old rules and paradigms turn out to be poor fits for this new environment.

WHAT FILTERS TRY TO DO

Internet filters are mechanical tools wrapped around subjective judgment. They are designed to block Internet content—usually content the company has identified and categorized. Some filters try to block keywords; some try to block individual sites; some try to block both.

THE REAL ISSUE IS SEX

Most filters are constructed to block many kinds of information, yet most libraries using filters "tweak" them to block only sexually-graphic information, and at that, some try to limit the content to that which is legally obscene (a fuzzy concept to grasp).

Discussions about filters share this emphasis; the focus is "porn," to quote many a message. Overall (though not exclusively) librarians are not terribly worried that someone might read an inaccurate recipe or see information provided about hate groups. For example, TIFAP volunteers commented several times that hate-related sites they found would help round out "all sides of an issue"—a wonderfully librarianesque response. (One definition of a librarian is someone who believes you can fix problems by throwing information at them.) On the other hand, most TIFAP volunteers, including librarians who ardently believed in the value of providing all other information, said that sexually-explicit information should be blocked on library computers, at least if it was visible as people walked by. Most librarians, it seems, aren't willing to go to the mat to defend the right of users to view pornography in library settings.

THE OTHER REAL ISSUE IS CHILDREN

As the TIFAP chapter also suggests, librarians often distinguish— as do other groups in our culture—between what is appropriate for children and what is appropriate for adults. When the media covers Internet content, nearly always the potential for children to view this content is raised at least once.

With traditional media, it is common for libraries to cede many decisions about children's access to their parents. On the Internet, there is no neat divide between "adult" and "child" collections, and furthermore, these descriptions have different meanings for each library that uses them. Finally, filters are not perfect, and cannot ensure that a child can't view a sexually-explicit site.

TEN DEBILITATING TRUISMS ABOUT INTERNET CONTENT AND FILTERS

We have a few debilitating truisms floating around librarianship (some of which I have been guilty of perpetrating). I'd like to air these before we launch into the technical discussions in this book.

1. Filters don't work right, anyway; they block phrases like "chicken breast."

I've said this myself, and I now stand partly corrected. The cheapest filters rely heavily on keyword blocking, and are inaccurate in both directions: they don't block what they say they do (human breasts can show up), but they block many other resources (sometimes even chicken breasts). The newer filters, however, which rely largely on human-identified lists of Internet sites, are much more precise—but none works perfectly.

2. Filters work great; all you have to do is tweak them a little.

Once performance issues with filters are largely resolved—and no filter worked perfectly (nor do responsible vendors claim otherwise)—the real problems with filters stand out in sharp relief. Most filters rely on proprietary site lists (databases might be more accurate) which the companies build at some expense, sometimes employing several dozen people to do nothing but scrutinize and categorize information. (None of the companies I talked to said they employed any librarians.) It is perfectly understandable, from a business perspective, why a company would want to keep this information private. However, these site lists privatize Internet content, placing control and accountability completely in the hands of an entity whose motivations are commercial, not service-oriented. This limits our quality-assurance capabilities, particularly with something as subjective as describing controversial content. This issue needs a lot of discussion in the library community. I do not know the solution, but I know we have a problem.

3. People can always view it elsewhere.

For some users, the library is the only place they will be able to use the Internet. United States Census data points out that you are much less likely to have access to a computer if you are poor, a person of color, do not have a college degree, or are unemployed. A walk through any poor urban area demonstrates that the library may easily be the only institution offering things middle-class Americans take for granted, such as bookstores, computers, ready access to copy machines, or simply a place for leisure reading.

4. The library should not act *in loco parentis*.

This is a fine ideal, but it speaks more to the socioeconomic status of the people who drafted this comment than it does to the realities of many library populations. Lower-income families in communities with few support services often direct their children to go to the library after school. Some librarians see this as a problem; others see it as opportunity; many see it as a fact of life.

The question is not whether libraries ever serve unsupervised children, or whether parents should or should not be there, but whether libraries can find ways to preserve their commitment to open access while meeting the expectations and needs of their communities.

5. There is one right answer to the filtering question.

We are naturally eager to demonstrate the validity of our decisions. The "how we done it right" article is a commonplace of library literature. When this translates to "you done it wrong," however, we stop learning. Some of the terribly tedious threads on the Internet have involved very defensive posturing on behalf of librarians who have made up their minds and can't entertain other concepts.

It would be more useful for all of us to develop better empathy for opposing viewpoints and decisions. Libraries that elect to use filters can learn from those who elect not to, and vice versa.

6. This Internet thing will blow over, anyway.

I was told this, not too long ago, by a practicing librarian. If you've bought this book, you know that comment is wrong; but what about the librarians who work with or for you?

7. The bad stuff is hard to find (alternatively, pornography is only X% of the Internet).

Nonsense. To provide one example, a TIFAP volunteer briefly engaged her teenage son as an evaluator of our questions. He typed "naked women" in a search engine and the results included many fine examples matching his search query. He, and his mother, were startled, though not upset; it disproved a truism they had heard. If you use the Internet at all, you know that stuff is "out there," and is very easy to locate.

I recently read an email message, duly making the rounds of the intellectual-freedom and library lists, which says that pornography is only 0.5% of all Internet content. There were 4,314,410 live hosts on the Internet as of July 1997 (Network Wizards, 1997). This is a very conservative figure, representing only those hosts that replied to a ping (an electronic "alive and well check"); nearly 20 million hostnames are registered by name. About 1700 websites are added daily (Quarterman, 1997). If .5% is accurate—and at present it is a word of mouth—this works out to about 21,000 pornographic hosts (not individual files), with 85 new hosts (again, not files) every day. While this isn't completely unmanageable, it's still a lot of data.

8. That Internet porn just pops up on the screen!

Even with all those explicit links, you still have to follow the links, nearly all the time. There is the possibility that a juvenile or inexpert user may not understand that "Sexy Babes XXX Hot Hot Hot!" refers to pornography, and in some cases the links may not be described. For the most part, however, sexually-explicit material does not "pop up" on screens any more than magazines or books strategically open themselves to selected pages.

9. PICS, or a collection-oriented tool, will make this problem moot.

Some have claimed the solution is in cataloging the entire Internet. One recent variation on that theme is Web rating systems, enabled by PICS, the Platform for Internet Content Selection, to which a brief chapter is devoted. I see PICS as yet one more variation on the filtering scheme, and one that, furthermore, will absorb a lot of tax dollars on the way.

There is one collection-oriented tool, a commercial product called The Library Channel, which I discuss in the product reviews. The fact that this software includes many blocking mechanisms speaks eloquently to the reality of cataloging the entire Internet.

10. I haven't had a problem, knock on wood.

The time to prepare for the Internet content issue is before it becomes a problem. It's hard to think with a gun at your head. Even if your community seems satisfied with your laissez-faire approach, there are nationally-funded organizations that specialize in pinpointing vulnerable communities where they can create challenges to library materials to push their own agendas. If nothing else, such a challenge will distract you from the work of delivering quality information, pleasure-reading, and library programming. At worst, you could find your choices dictated from government agencies at the city, county, or state level.

Less dramatically, but more common, is the rush-decision made on the heels of a precipitating incident, such as a teenager complaining to her parent that she "accidentally" came across sexually-explicit information on a library computer. The monitoring capabilities of some filters, or a monitoring tool, could keep you primed with information ahead of time, so you can speak to how often or infrequently this has actually occurred in your library. How much is too much is, again, your call. (If you want an easy career, go into neurosurgery or air traffic control; these days, librarianship is tough.)

This doesn't mean you should rush out to buy a filter. Far from it! If you are truly opposed to using filters, now is the time to prepare your strategy. If you have considered using a filter, begin evaluating them so you won't find yourself pushed into a bad decision. Even if you are completely ready and interested in selecting an Internet filter, working on this project now, on your schedule, may have a deterrent effect. More than one library has emailed me to say that selective use of filters was designed as a deterrent to more intervention. Whether or not this is the right approach for your community is for you to decide.

WHAT WOULD I DO? WHAT DO I THINK?

When I asked Frank Bridge, senior computer person at Austin Public Library, what his advice was for libraries considering filters, he said, "make a decision, and take your lumps." That about sums up my attitude. I think we should all be given enough rope to hang ourselves—that is, if you want to filter content, all right; if you don't, that's all right too. I'm biased toward open access, and I'm biased toward the democratic process, but I'm particularly fond of accountability and personal responsibility.

I am more concerned about outsourcing decisions about what's blocked to a third, commercial, party: the filter's producers. I recognize—as I have not always recognized—that one, two, or three librarians with real jobs can't create a working list of all the really bad pornography sites. On the other hand, I am not ready to stop worrying and love Internet filters. Again, democracy and accountability: in our culture, we employ elaborate checks and balances to ensure both. I don't want assurances from a vendor; I want to shine light on the information. That's one reason I am donating 10% of my royalties from this book to Voters Telecommunications Watch, http://www.vtw.org, a good-government group, towards establishing a newsletter on intellectual freedom issues. I too believe we can solve problems by throwing information at them—the more the merrier.

There's an old expression among Internet aficionados: "information wants to be free." People sometimes interpret this to mean that authors should not charge for their work, or that copyright should be ignored. What this expression means, in the most classic sense, is that information wants to be accessible. We deserve freedom of information, and even more importantly, so do our communities. Nobody cares about this issue as much as we do, and we, the library profession, will have to shoulder most of the effort of raising consciousness on this issue, educating people again and again on the relationship between information and democracy, and implementing procedures and technologies that help preserve these freedoms. How we get there is open to discussion. The first thing we must do is get educated, and that's why I wrote this book.

PART I:
ESSENTIAL BACKGROUND

1

What Filters Are and How They Work

Note that this chapter is different from chapter 2, "Types of Filtering Software," designed to acquaint you with different software versions. Here I'm going to walk you through the different types of content blocked by Internet filters.

KEYWORD BLOCKING

Filters using keyword blocking employ a pre-defined word list of supposedly objectionable terms; these lists can usually be modified to add or delete entries. These terms are nearly always related to sexuality, human biology or sexual orientation, such as XXX, sexual, queer, penis, vagina, pussy, and so forth, though Cybersitter also blocks terms such as "death" and Cyber Patrol, with keyword blocking enabled, even blocks the term "pain."

Keyword blocking, in the jargon of filter vendors, is referred to variously as "content identification," "content analysis," "Dynamic Document Review," "phrase blocking," or just, simply, "keyword blocking." Despite these fancy names, keyword blocking does not function as advertised; as one TIFAP tester said of Cybersitter's claim to be context-sensitive, "nothing could be further from the truth." Websites of poems, medical information, children's rhymes, and news releases were summarily blocked based on simple pattern-matching, and all terms had the presumption of prurience or ill-use—they were, however innocent, *a priori* labeled as objectionable.

Because keyword blocking works so poorly, the question you need to ask is not whether the filter offers it, but whether this feature can be disabled. Many librarians consider keyword blocking to be ineffectual, but still it turns up. Even I-Gear, which employs a very sophisticated keyword analysis tool, Dynamic Document Review, tripped up on search terms with this feature enabled. The vendors, in response to our queries, replied that it was a flaw in the algorithm that was then fixed. My two cents on this is to test this feature yourself because I'm not convinced this problem *can* be fixed. I-Gear's heritage is Sun, a big company with many notches in its belt, but if these programmers have found the magic bullet for content recognition, the rest of the information science community has been remarkably complacent about this news.

If Keyword Blocking Doesn't Work, Why Is It There?

Keyword filtering relies on some fairly naive assumptions. The first assumption is that words never have more than one meaning. The word "Roger" is never blocked, though in Australia that word is also slang for penis; the word "cock" is often blocked, although it has several meanings—not only slang for the term penis, but a verb associated with guns and a noun associated with birds.

What happens when a filter accesses a keyword it is trying to block? We discovered in TIFAP that with keyword blocking enabled, a filter identifying an offending word in the body of the poem would do one of four things, depending on the filter: stop the file in transit, display the file but obscure the targeted term, deliver some but not all of the file, or (calamitously) shut down the browser or even the computer. Additionally, display of the file is often slowed down because the filter is searching the file for occurrences of the term.

In TIFAP, we demonstrated over and over again that keyword blocking seriously hinders information retrieval; when we disabled keyword blocking and tried URLs that had been blocked, information retrieval improved significantly. At least one version of the poem, "pussycat, pussycat," was blocked by every filter that enables keyword blocking. With keyword blocking disabled, none of these sites were blocked.

Why, then, is keyword blocking a feature in many filters? It's no accident that the least expensive filters offer keyword blocking as a way to bolster how much information is blocked. Not all filters block all protocols. Unix-based firewall filters commonly only block http, leaving gopher, ftp, irc, and other protocols "clear channel" (or undisturbed, in the jargon of proxy server vendors). Site selection is expensive in terms of labor hours, as anyone familiar with its distant relative, cataloging, can understand. But even more sophisticated and expensive tools offer keyword blocking because site identification has one major weakness: a site cannot be blocked unless people know about it, and hundreds of new sites appear daily. Keyword blocking is the only "line of defense" against any Website that has not been manually identified by a human content selector.

Finally, some vendors sincerely believe that keyword blocking will someday be effective. The I-Gear vendor wasn't snowing me when he said his product performs sophisticated word counts; it does—I've seen the calculations. I think, on some level, the I-Gear vendor was right; algorithm here, algorithm there, and pretty soon you have artificial intelligence. However, in a rigorous information retrieval environment, these tools don't work well enough today, and that's what matters.

To understand the occasional quandary the limits to the two methods of blocking can entail, consider DejaNews (http://www.dejanews.com). DejaNews is a web-based interface and search engine for Usenet, the service that provides discussion groups (also called newsgroups) on thousands of topics. Usenet has for over a decade been a freewheeling environment representing the vast spectrum of human interest, from highly scientific discussions, to easygoing chatter and heated arguments. Usenet also carries discussions, and distribution, of more controversial issues, such as bomb-building and child pornography (information also available elsewhere on the Web, of course).

Some libraries believe in blocking anything related to "chat" in a library setting, which would cover DejaNews from several perspectives. But let's say, for the sake of argument, that this doesn't describe your library, or you think the content in DejaNews is important enough to rule out blocking it completely.

If you enable keyword blocking, you will have far too much "friendly fire" from the good information you block. I have yet to see a filter that would enable keyword blocking for one site, and the tradeoff would still be loss of information (for example, the next time you wanted to take a picture of a child). Even the most "sophisticated" filter can't enable keyword blocking for a single site.

Understand that the problem is not Usenet, but the fact that these groups are carried into a web interface via DejaNews. If your filter blocks NNTP (Usenet) groups, or if you're lucky enough to be your own Internet Service Provider and carry your own NNTP (Usenet) feed, that's nice, because you can define which groups you will receive, but it's irrelevant from the perspective of the DejaNews problem—it's a web resource. You could also disable Usenet at the packet-filter level, but that also would accomplish nothing with respect to DejaNews. You could, however, decide to receive selected newsgroups in lieu of DejaNews. You'd lose the powerful DejaNews search capability, but you would still have the groups you felt useful.

If you're expecting an answer to this problem, I don't have one—except that hard cases make bad law!

Keyword blocking technologies are also used to assist companies with site blocking, as described below.

SITE BLOCKING: NOT QUITE PRECISE

Site blocking means that humans identify Internet sites, which are placed into access or denial lists (depending on whether people do or do not want others to access the site). Throughout this book I refer to site lists, which are almost always denial lists at the vendor level (except for The Library Channel).

Pay careful note to the technical abilities and the intent of the vendor. Some filters are able to block to the file level; some can only block top-level domains. When you test the filter, observe what happens to domains carrying a mixed bag of information.

In most products, site lists are organized into arbitrary categories. The purpose of these categories is to provide the consumer more choice, and indeed two products migrating from the K-12 environment, Bess and I-Gear, realized the importance of categories for the library market and are enabling categories.

Site list categories sometimes read like a laundry-list of human concerns and interests, with some venal sins thrown in. Some filters have as few as 6 (Surfwatch) and others as many as 29 (Websense). Having extensive categories is particularly true for companies that market their product to the business arena, where the objective may be to prevent workers from accessing information that libraries have traditionally specialized in sharing, such as sports, hobbies, entertainment, humor, and newsworthy issues. Ironically, sometimes filter companies classify and block information libraries pay good money to locate, such as "Alternative Journals" (Smart Filter) and "Activist Groups" (Websense).

Though the site lists sometimes share vaguely common areas, there is no MARC-like standard for classifying sites. You can count on one or several categories related to sexual activity, and another for criminal activity, such as bomb-making, and one for chat. Sites related to homosexuality might be singled out in an area called "Sexuality/Lifestyles" (Websense) or "Lifestyle" (Smart Filter), or lumped in with "Adult" (I-Gear), or sprinkled throughout content categories (Surfwatch).

The lack of granularity in the area of sexual information is something TIFAP testers commented on. Despite the attempts of these companies to distinguish among obscene, explicit, hard-core, and other similar terms, there seems to be a few thousand sites most people at least agree are extremely sexually explicit, and several more tiers of sites that push various buttons depending on the audience and the setting.

Site Selection: An Art, Not a Science

Identifying all potentially questionable content on the Internet sounds daunting, given the vast sea that is the Internet. It is, but the selectors have automated tools to help them identify Internet content. For example, software robots may scrub the Internet for new files, then flag files which have content known to be common to the files they are attempting to block and/or categorize. Content classifiers also monitor search engines, discussion groups, and other tools for locating new content.

The analogy in our profession is the technical services department of a large library, with collection-development librarians identifying resources and catalogers making decisions about access points. (Of course, the analogy is awry, since we expend our labor to *provide* access to information, and we are educated information professionals.)

There are two problems (at least) that can arise in site selection activities.

First, files may slip by if they do not have any content resembling what is being flagged or have any other reason to be blocked. In TIFAP we noticed that the farther the content strayed from pornography, the less precise the filters were. For example, Websense, which was relatively good with denying sexually-explicit sites while not blocking "good" sites, seemed to be unaware of about half of the chat sites our tester retrieved with chat blocking enabled.

I have two theories about the sloppier blocking outside of the areas related to sexuality. One: pornography is the real target, and the other categories, however elaborate, are more perfunctory because people don't care as much. Two: we have a richer, more precise vocabulary for sexual behavior than we do for a concept as diffuse and new as "chat." Software retrieval tools would therefore not be as precise at identifying chat sites. These concepts are not mutually exclusive, of course.

It is well-known that as search engines develop fancy algorithms for locating information, enterprising content developers quickly find ways to outfox the search engines to make their information rank higher in relevance. This is a cat-and-mouse game with no end in sight (though I suppose we can say that it will lead to more sophisticated content analysis tools).

The other problem with site selection is the issue of friendly fire. It is possible to block a lot of good content without malicious intent if other material on the website meets the company's blocking criteria. An interesting story about a man's liver transplant was blocked by one filter because the company had classified the site by its top-level files, which were pornographic. Though in theory most companies can block to the file level—a feature noted in the product reviews—because these companies are busy identifying what to block, they may not always look closely at a website's subdirectories if the top directory meets the blocking criteria.

Local Site Lists

Local access and deny lists are used in filters to override the settings provided by the vendor in its site database. Vendors talk to librarians about local access and deny lists, unaware that for generations we have had first-hand knowledge of the consequences of a database that we could not put all information into. These lists are stopgap measures that, however necessary, underscore the highly proprietary "one size fits all" nature of the databases they modify after the fact.

PROTOCOL BLOCKING

Protocol blocking means denying access to all the resources of a particular type of Internet service—for example, to disable access to telnet, ftp, gopher, Internet Relay Chat (irc), or Usenet. Note that on networks, disabling this service can usually be accomplished at the router level.

In libraries, the justifications for disabling these protocols are usually resource allocation and security. For the first justification, a resource is perceived to be too bandwidth-intensive to maintain or too over-used by one group (such as teenagers) to even bother with. For the second, security issues—often combined with low use—may prompt a response from on high or at the local level. On high, a system administrator may disable a service he or she believes (perhaps from monitoring network traffic over a period) a low-use, forgotten resource, since this is a tempting hole for a digital bandit to break into. On the local level, librarians may decide that the hassles and security issues involved with downloading or telnet access are not worth the trouble. From listening to traffic on PUBLIB and other discussion groups, there is quite often a long and persuasive story to justify disabling a protocol; if you don't have a reason, you may ask yourself why you are doing it (or you may decide if it ain't broke, don't fix it).

Note that many types of these resources are becoming integrated into the Web; disabling irc has no effect on web-based chat.

All content-blocking filters I have looked at steer clear of blocking mail-related protocols. On the other hand, it appears that with the standalone version of Netscape Communicator 4.03, we finally have a browser that does not include email capabilities. Combine this with a workstation security tool such as Ikiosk to prevent users from installing their own email software on your system (http://www. hypertec.com, 1-800-663-8381, about $25 per workstation), you can limit everything except web-based email, which some filters may exclude or you may not consider a problem.

TIME BLOCKING

Most filters are able to limit access by time of day, and sometimes combine this with type of protocol. As discussed elsewhere in this book, this can be useful if resource-allocation issues require you to limit a popular feature at peak times because you can continue to offer the resource at other times.

Not one filter to date, however, has implemented the feature librarians mention on discussion lists: limiting access by time-outs, such as ending a user session after 30 minutes. While other software tools such as Fortres are often used for this purpose, it would seem logical to seek this in one integrated tool (versus purchasing separate software, which amplifies your chances for software conflict problems). This is a feature I have discussed with vendors, who have indicated interest. It is a feature that could work in conjunction with client or user blocking to ensure everyone had a "fair share" with a limited resource. (It might also be a good resource to be able to schedule, so that patrons who came to the library at off-hours could enjoy uninterrupted sessions.)

CLIENT BLOCKING

For those of you not conversant in computer jargon, clients, to filter vendors, mean workstations, not humans. In libraries, client blocking can be used to determine access levels at specific locations, such as the children's room, the adult services area, and so forth. Additionally, tracking information about client network activity can provide useful reporting information.

Most server-based products can control workstation access at the workstation level, by IP (Internet Protocol) access. The level of access can vary from filter enabled or disabled, to very specific configuration of each workstation, and in some filters you can create groups to facilitate uniform access levels for a specific area.

USER BLOCKING

Most filter vendors with background in the business and educational markets are familiar with users who sit in front of the same workstation all day. The notion of a library patron who comes into a building at random times, stands at any old computer, and is entitled to specific services—and might even expect remote support—is new to most of these vendors. Add other types of user blocking common in libraries, such as identifying juvenile versus adult users, or (to add a complex, but realist twist) juvenile-with-adult-consent, juvenile-without-adult consent, adult, out-of-county, guest, and so-seriously-delinquent-we-are-denying-all-services-til-they-pony-up-the-dough, and you have an environment that has left vendors speechless, with me listening to silence crackling across long-distance phone lines.

This is our world, though, and providing custom access at the user level, and letting parents be as digitally *in parentis* as they can be, given the limits of the technology, could be a great peacemaker for many communities torn over issues of access and the Internet.

I'd like to see more filters supporting patrons logging in at their user levels, if such a thing exists for the library in question. This would allow libraries with limited computers or a very nomadic population to let patrons access information at levels that are fairly predictable and intentional, with the caveats, of course, that filters are not perfect and nothing is guaranteed.

A couple of filters offered support for extensive lists of users, and in at least one product as of this writing the list can be imported in a variety of formats. That's not quite real-time, and it's more work, but it's better than nothing. Jerry Kuntz, in his survey to filter vendors, asked them if they could support querying the patron database of OPACs. This was a good question, and it was met with a good answer, when I discussed it with vendors: it would depend on the OPAC. If the OPAC had an API[1] for its patron database, that would at least start the process. In the meantime, expect to see more and more filters offering support for patron identification. Every vendor I spoke to about this said barcode support would be fairly trivial, and would be implemented if market demand warranted it. I-Gear already offers the capability to read in a user list exported in several formats. When I added that most library patrons often log into other databases by keying in barcode numbers because most workstations don't have barcode readers, vendors were surprised, but added that there was no reason why a patron database couldn't use barcode numbers for its user identification.

Additionally, the notion of types of access is foreign to some filter vendors. Some filters assume a central administrator who makes all decisions. However, in many library environments, quite a few decisions about information access are delegated to the degreed professionals who work on the front lines of library service and are going to be the first to know when, for example, a filter has blocked information needed to answer a question. The abilities to override blocks and to add or delete sites, while limiting access to administering or reconfiguring the system, is a type of user access that should be watched for carefully.

WEB RATING SYSTEMS SUCH AS PICS

PICS is discussed in its own brief chapter, *Web Rating Systems*, due to the length and specificity of this topic. Note, however, that on the one hand, all vendors were either ready for PICS or soon would be; on the other hand, they considered PICS a "market check-off" as a current non-issue. I don't disagree, as of this writing.

The type of software often determines how well the capabilities in this chapter are enabled, or if they are even present. Accordingly, our next discussion will be about the types of software currently available for Internet content filters.

NOTES

1. An API is an application programming interface: a set of programming functions which can be used to interact with another program.

2

Types of Filtering Software

In this chapter we will walk through the three major types of filter software, and the variations available within these categories.

There are five major types of filter software:

> **Filter Software Types**
>
> **Client software**, for individual workstations
>
> **LAN-based software**, for network installations of client software
>
> **Standalone proxy server software**, which serves as an Internet gateway for the server
>
> **Proxy server "plug-ins,"** which work in conjunction with existing proxy-server software
>
> **Firewall software**, which sits on a Unix firewall

Additionally, three other types of services warrant a close look:

> **Three Other Filter Types**
>
> Remote proxy servers
>
> Pre-packaged "proxy in a box" servers
>
> Filtering through an ISP

I've grouped all eight types by function, but it's more useful to discuss them in terms of affordability and capability, starting from the most low-cost, low-demand solutions to network-wide solutions.

Generally, the filter types exhibit common performance traits within their categories. Don't assume that the client, proxy or firewall version of the "same" product will be similar; they may seem like completely different products!

CLIENT SOFTWARE

Client software is installed on individual computers (known also as clients or workstations).

In addition to being one of three solutions for very limited, client-only settings such as small libraries, client software can also be a way to use filters selectively, rather than imposing them across an entire system. The cost-effectiveness of clients diminishes with the number of workstations; you can factor under $50 per computer per year, but that is also before you factor in the effort to maintain them.

Filters that are primarily client-based, such as Surfwatch, Cybersitter and Cyber Patrol, have attracted a lot of attention, in part because some of them are notoriously poor performers, in part because they likely have a wider installed user base. Despite the bad press, don't rule out all client software. One package, Cyber Patrol, tweaked to minimal settings and with keyword worked adequately, with the caveats that it blocked some "good stuff" and let through some "bad stuff," has limited reporting, and will require maintenance and perhaps several reinstallations during its life cycle. It is far from a perfect product, but depending on the scenario, it might be right for you. It will cost you labor hours to maintain these tools, and their limited capabilities create work ably handled by their more powerful counterparts—but all in all, if you don't have many computers, or you do not have dedicated Internet access, client software may be your best solution.

One very important tip about client filters: always note, and follow, deinstallation steps very carefully. They are designed to wreak havoc with computers if they are simply deleted from the systems. Remove them with the program deinstallation program, and if you have any questions, contact the vendor before you start.

> **What are proxy servers?**
>
> Proxy servers redirect all input to and from your Internet server through a third-party (or "proxy") server.

REMOTE PROXY SERVERS

Remote proxy servers are another option for smaller settings or limited filtering. For 25 users, a ballpark price, right now, would be under $25 per workstation, making them cheaper than client software, and that's before calculating the maintenance savings.

Remote proxy servers are subscription services where you pass all Internet requests through a vendor's server. Bess is an example of a remote proxy server (though you can also license a "proxy in a box" solution through their company, N2H2). While Bess, at the time of evaluation, missed several features that we would expect in a library setting, particularly the ability to selectively enable categories, it also offered some features appealing where technical support is limited, not the least of which is the lack of software-maintenance overhead or performance problems associated with maintaining client software. Typically, all you need to do is configure each browser to point to the remote proxy server (and yes, these companies have thought through all the devious methods people know for bypassing proxy servers). Combined with remote administration capabilities, remote proxy servers are a tidy "white-glove" approach to proxied services.

A performance note: to work well, remote proxy servers must be robust enough to meet user demand, so you do not "bottleneck" at the proxy server during busy periods. This means as a company expands, it should also expand the number of computers available for this support. If and when other companies offer remote proxy services, and you are comparing the two products, ask how many users and how many and what type of servers, and compare ratios. You will still get your best information from current users, but this preliminary information may help frame the questions you ask.

I asked a number of vendors if they were considering remote proxy service. Their responses suggested that they would take their cues from market demand.

FILTERING THROUGH AN ISP

Some Internet Service Providers (ISPs) are beginning to offer filtered access to Internet services for their customers, for a few dollars more per month than basic service. (In fact, some of the companies noted in this book, including Websense, are selling this service to ISPs.)

If, to paraphrase Pooh, you were a library of very small means, filtered service through an ISP could be your least expensive solution. Furthermore, like remote proxy services (which this service is in a sense, anyway), you are spared the computer maintenance issues. Filtered ISP services are just coming available, and the unknowns include how configurable the service is at your end and how well it works overall. I also wonder how well filtering works removed one more step from the company that maintains the (private, encrypted) site lists. I do think it will be very low overhead for you financially to find out; just don't commit for a lengthy time period until you have used the service and know it meets your needs.

LAN-BASED SOFTWARE

It speaks volumes that only one product, Cyber Patrol, offers a networked version of their client software. The one systems librarian I know who has lived with this product for a year reported extensive conflicts with other software programs and labor-intensive maintenance issues. His system is not renewing its license, and they are currently testing other solutions.

In all fairness, I think LAN-based software solutions were developed in a time, long ago (1995) when most organizations did not see Internet services as a distribution platform as much as they do today. It was a solution designed around current business practice.

PROXY-IN-A-BOX SERVERS

Some vendors, such as Bess and X-Stop, market a "canned" solution. This proxy-in-a-box is commonly a Unix-based server preconfigured for filtering with the vendor's product. The company will often provide services to come in on-site and configure the server. Though the server is Unix-based, it should be blind to your system (the jargon one vendor used was that "it could be dropped in as an Ethernet device").

This type of service may be relatively painless for systems large enough to support networked services but still limited in their technical capabilities. If you are thinking of going this route, however, ask the vendor whether you can return the product (or within what timeframe you can return it) if you are not happy with it, since you can't really test a canned solution until it is in place.

STANDALONE PROXY SERVERS AND PROXY SERVER PLUG-INS

Proxy servers are used at sites with internal Internet services. Nearly all are Windows NT based. They can cost as little as under $5 per workstation per year, depending on the number of licenses, and even the smallest licenses, such as a 25–user pack, can be cost effective compared to other small-scale solutions.

Although maintaining a proxy server requires skilled automation support, the word in the street is that these are not troublesome tools to support, for the most part. At their best, they are nearly transparent in terms of impact on system services, easy to configure at the system level, and as discussed above, cost-effective per workstation.

I have noticed that server-based filters that "grew up" with a K-12 or business customer base tend to be limited in levels of access—for example, in providing a password override for reference librarians—since they have been designed around one set of organizational imperatives. As these products adapt to the library environment, where we all have varying stakes in information services, we can expect them to support more of the library-oriented features discussed in chapter 3, "Filter Features."

Like most software, proxy servers perform best with plenty of elbow room (hard drive space and memory), so they can manage all the routing, rerouting, address translation and logging activities without bogging down Internet services. They often have additional hardware, software and configuration requirements (such as a recent version of NT, two Network Interface Cards, or similar thresholds of support).

Some of these products administer their services through a web-based interface, in part to enable remote administration.

Standalone Proxy Server

A standalone proxy server is different from proxy server plug-ins in that it serves as the gateway to the Internet for the library's server. Because so much is depending on this one piece of software, its performance should be carefully studied before a final purchase decision is made, and it should be configured very carefully.

Proxy Server Plug-Ins

These filters are designed to work as companion software to existing proxy servers on your system. Most of the time this means either the Microsoft or Netscape proxy server, but in researching this book I found several other products, such as Oracle's proxy server. Note that you will have to license the proxy server separately, if you don't have one already; the Microsoft Proxy Server was $999 in early September 1997, so this is not a trivial expense.

Some of the capabilities of proxy-server plug-ins will be colored by the respective capabilities of the proxy server they depend on. However, there may be very little performance difference in look-and-feel or performance between a standalone and plug-in filter; Websense, for example, can be configured to do either job, and has the same interface in either case. They are also not supporting Internet gateway services, so they can concentrate on their primary job, blocking Internet content.

Unix Firewall Filters

These are installed at the firewall level, require a fairly high level of automation support, typically block only http (Web) requests.

To be frank, I have very little knowledge about these products; most companies that produce an NT product have a Unix firewall product. When possible, I included vendor-supplied product information for the firewall versions of the filters evaluated for this book.

3
Filter Features

INTRODUCTION

Whether or not you are thinking about using a filter, understanding filters and how they work is essential. You can use the information in this chapter to guide you in making the following choices:

1. Using a specific filter
2. Using a specific configuration of a filter
3. Not using filters

Additionally, this information can help you build your knowledge base so you can talk to the issue of filters. You may even want to initiate discussion for staff or your community, perhaps through a library program, if you sense being proactive on this issue would be beneficial. (Whether it is better to let sleeping dogs lie is something your intuition, knowledge, and experience will guide you on.)

Will this information change? Of course! Not only that, the rate of change is very rapid in the Internet software world. For new, modified or obsolesced features, see the book's Website at:

http://www.bluehighways.com/filters/

However, some information is constant. Software performance issues, for example, are crucial, and regardless of what version you're dealing with, you need to determine if the product interferes with other programs, crashes, or slows down your network.

All the many features combine to create four major characteristics:

A filter, to be useful and appropriate in a library setting, should ideally:

➢ Block what you want it to—and only what, where, and when you want it to

➢ Let you see what's blocked

➢ Let you change what's blocked

➢ Not create extra work or muck with your computer system

No software program is perfect, and it's not reasonable to expect filters to be perfect. Not all problems with filters, however, have technical fixes. Letting you see what's blocked is a problem because vendors spend money to create the lists of blocked sites. That doesn't mean it's not a good goal, though, or something we shouldn't have in the back of our minds even as we implement a less-than-perfect tool.

1. SOFTWARE CAPABILITIES

1A Client or Server-based Software

As discussed in Chapter 1, "What Filters Are and How They Work," some software is **client** (meaning it is installed on a local computer) and some is **server-based** (meaning the software is installed at the network level and is transparent to individual computers). Client software, from word processing to Web browsers, is common in settings where standalone computers are used (a small library, a home office), while server-based software is more common in larger systems.

While I lump most discussion of server-based software under that label, server-based software can take several forms:

Table: Filter Features

- "Watch for this feature" means it should be coming out soon—perhaps by the time you read this page!

		Feature	Found in any filter?
1		Feature	Found in any filter?
	A	Client or server-based software	All are one or the other
	B	Shared remote proxy servers	One; watch for this feature •
	C	Filter "box" available	Most server-based solutions
	D	Filter fail-safe in case filter fails	Some
	E	Monitor vs. block	Some clients, more server-based filters
	F	Reporting capabilities	Most
	G	Remote administration	Some server-based tools
2	A	Filter blocks *all* targeted content	No
	B	Filter blocks *only* targeted content	No
	C	Keyword blocking can be disabled	Most
	D	Filter blocks/allows to file level	Most
	E	Hostnames resolve to IP address	Many
3	A	Extensive site list	Some more than others
	B	List of blocked sites is viewable	Very few
	C	List of blocked sites is editable	Some
	D	Supports local access/deny lists	Some
	E	Supports shared lists	Some
	F	Supports third-party lists	Some
	G	Supports customized lists	None (though perhaps on request)
	H	Site list updated automatically	Some
	I	Site list is maintained daily	Some

4	**A**	Block by protocol	Most
	B	Block by time	Some
	C	Support time-out	No; watch for this feature •
	D	Multiple configuration options	Several; watch for this feature •
	E	Patron can access by barcode	None; watch for this feature •
	F	Filter supports warn-versus-block	Some
5	**A**	Site list arranged in categories	Most
	B	Categories can be selectively enabled	Most
	C	Filter supports library-defined categories	Some
	D	Categories correspond with LCSH	None
	E	Site list supports local holdings	None
6	**A**	Recommend changes to master list	Nearly all
	B	Strong user diagnostics and feedback	Some
	C	PICS support	Some; watch for this feature •
	D	Patron notice cannot be disabled	Some

➤ Standalone proxy servers installed on an Internet server
➤ Software used in conjunction with existing proxy servers
➤ Network versions of client products (not really "server-based," but close enough)
➤ Preconfigured hardware and software packages (the "proxy in a box" solution)

You may have a good idea of whether you need client or server-based software. A small library with standalone computers will first look at client software, while a large library with a local area network and dedicated Internet connection will first look at server-based products, but there are some scenarios where the choice may not be obvious.

Note that capabilities of the same product can change—sometimes dramatically—between versions (such as Windows 3.1 and Windows 95, or Netscape proxy and standalone proxy). There can also be variations between client and server versions of the product, and sometimes even among client versions of the product. This is very true for filter software; when you read the product reviews, heed carefully which version I'm describing.

As you read the product reviews in this book, you will note that overall, server-based solutions tend to outperform client-based filters in most areas. The convenient analogy in the library profession is the library catalog. You know that if you buy catalog software for a very tiny library—say, your church or temple library—it will be a much more limited product than if you are looking at very robust, system-wide solutions such as those sold by Ameritech or DRA. For the same reasons, this is also true for filter products. Client-based products aren't as powerful, nor do they have as much technology invested in them.

Library systems with a computer network will occasionally have to consider client-based solutions. Austin Public Library, for example, has an arrangement between the library and a local community network that precludes use of server-based solutions, and predictably, maintaining 50 copies of client software (in this case, Cyber Patrol) is difficult. Frank Bridge, their chief computer person, noted that maintaining these computers was like cutting a lawn with a pair of scissors—by the time you get to one end it's time to start over from the beginning!

On the other hand, if the "hot spot" is confined to one or two computers in a specific area, installing a server-based solution may be overkill, particularly from a cost perspective—though remote proxy servers are another consideration.

Software performance is another area where you really must talk to people who have been using (for at least a few months) the filter you're looking at, and get your computer support person in on this discussion as well.

In general, server-based software outperforms client software, at least from the TIFAP experience and from all anecdotal evidence. However, some server-based programs have had reports of serious network problems compounded by poor technical support and documentation. One library system reported significant problems with Cyber Patrol's network version, so much so that after one year they chose not to renew the software license.

Several of the client programs created significant problems for testers through the testing period. These were the kinds of problems that crop up when you have been using a program for weeks or months, not just a quick look on a Friday afternoon: conflicts with other software, difficulty in installation and removal, freezes, and so forth. Net Nanny, Cybersitter and Cyber Snoop had very poor software performance in TIFAP testing. Cyber Patrol testers did not report any problems, but two library systems that use the client version of this product report that they frequently need to re-install this software.

Cybersitter and Net Nanny also had very annoying behavior when the tester accessed material the filter deemed objectionable. Tools designed to prevent users from typing "bad" words either covered words with XXXs or obliterated them. In Cybersitter, terms such as *butt*, *sexual*, and *death* were all susceptible to these features, but Net Nanny also (and inconsistently) X'ed out notes from testers to me in forms they were attempting to fill out, and popped up as interference in word processing programs as well. Clearly, disabling these features is key, but so is understanding that they are useless to begin with in a real information setting—that they are really "market check-off items," as one vendor called them, to appeal to the home buyer worried that his child might be reading (or typing) foul language. Not surprisingly, these types of problems do not appear in the server-based products.

Ease of configuration also varied. The client software was surprisingly complicated for single-purpose tools. To configure Cyber Patrol's client software to block only sexually explicit content took some testers several tries, even after one tester wrote a page of separate instructions. The Library Channel had one feature, "domain surfing," that was not explained in context, requiring the tester to consult the documentation frequently. I was never able to remove Cybersitter from my work computer, and ultimately requested, with bowed head, a reinstallation of my computer's operating system.

Server-based software requires expertise to install, of course, but the systems librarians I spoke to who had experience with filters said most of the tools were easy enough, from their point of view. I read the documentation for the server-based products and found most of it straightforward. Administration of Bess, which I had server access to, was extremely simple (though that is partly because many features of the version of Bess I was evaluating are controlled by the main company).

1B Shared Remote Proxy Servers

The economies of scale may suggest that very small libraries or libraries that want filtering software on a small percentage of computers should not consider a server-based filter. However, don't rule this out completely. There are two possibilities for making server-based solutions available to small libraries.

For small libraries, one possibility is a consortial purchase; you could belong to a group, such as a library network, that goes in together to license a product. If you are considering a consortial purchase, ask how much local control you will have over the filter regarding what and how it blocks. If configuration of the filter, including what it blocks, will be controlled from a central office, ask yourself if you're comfortable with whoever is doing the selection.

Another option is to license a shared remote-proxy product, such as Bess offers. A shared proxy server is a server located at the company's computer site through which you redirect Internet requests for each computer you license. As of this writing, the least expensive version of Bess was a shared proxy server that was not an ideal library product, since its categories could not be selectively enabled and keyword blocking could not be disabled. However, the potential exists for any company to offer remote-proxy service for small customers, and the Bess company says they are considering establishing a "library edition" of their shared proxy server which would be configured with the preferences they hear libraries asking for.

1C Filter "Box" Available ("Proxy in a Box")

Some vendors offer a preconfigured server which is then dropped into the computer network. Sometimes the company comes on site and configures the software. In this sense, preconfigured servers fall in between remote proxy servers and installed software in ease of support and configurability.

1D Filter Fail-Safe in Case Filter Fails

A very interesting question to ask is whether you can get to the Internet if the product isn't working. If you have your system configured to go through a tool that is a standalone proxy server, and the proxy server fails, the answer is no. Whether this is a real problem or not is unknown; anecdotal evidence suggests otherwise, but I do like to stay up late at night thinking up worst-case scenarios!

1E Monitor vs. Block
1F Reporting Capabilities

Monitoring is an extremely useful tool for identifying what you want to block—or whether you want to block. Monitoring means that the filter reports all traffic, classifies it by the filter's categories,but does not block any traffic. The reports are broken down by time and workstation, feature detailed reporting on individual sites, and thus are very good for analyzing what is actually going on.

The decision to filter is often initiated by a precipitating incident. This incident may be "just the tip of the iceberg." On the other hand, it may be the whole iceberg, or at least a good chunk of it. You only know if you measure. Only you can decide what your "incident tolerance" is, but armed with more information, you can at least speak to the issue.

Think of monitoring as a key decision-making tool for configuring what you block. You may want to track types of traffic at some workstations—in the children's room or in computers facing public areas. If use of a resource such as chat is peaking during times when library bandwidth is already in short supply (such as late afternoon), you may be able to fine-tune resource allocation so chat is available when other resources are not consuming your computing resources.

Reporting is also a very important tool for understanding how the filter is performing in real life. Through reports, you can see what is blocked and what is not blocked, on a per-workstation basis. This information needs to be balanced with the need for patron privacy and, like other patron information, guarded carefully, but keep in mind that if users cannot access needed resources because filters are blocking them, you need to know this. While feedback tools are good for reporting inappropriately blocked resources, we know enough about user behavior to recognize that users encountering blocked sites are more often than not going to work around the problem, particularly if the library has indicated that it is blocking "bad" resources. It isn't typical behavior for someone to approach a librarian and say, "you know that resource you think I shouldn't see? I want to see it." Clearly, you also will want to scrutinize the reports very carefully during any pre-purchase evaluation period.

If you are not the person who maintains your library's system, ask your technical person to look at the filter's reporting capabilities. Reporting capabilities all sound alike in the sales ads, but vary widely in actual usefulness. At minimum, these reports should tell you, by workstation, what URLs have been accessed, what URLs have been blocked, what categories the blocks were in, and the full URL of the blocked resource. Reports that only provide IP addresses for the URLs accessed and blocked (see 2E, below, for an explanation of IP addresses) are not nearly as useful as reports that provide the full "alphabetical" address.

In addition to looking for monitoring capabilities in filters, note that two products, Cyber Snoop and On Guard, reviewed in brief in this book, are designed specifically for monitoring Internet activity.

1G Remote Administration

If you maintain the library system, you know why I bring this up. If you don't, your computer support staff will tell you: so they can peek at the system from time-to-time over nights, weekends, and holidays and if necessary start, stop, or reconfigure it as required. This feature is available in several server-based products.

2. BLOCKING PRECISION

The connection between filter performance and keyword blocking is so close that the first three features (2A, 2B, and 2C) are discussed together below.

The ideal filter blocks what you want blocked—no more, no less. The ideal filter doesn't exist—not by a long shot. However, there are wide variations in filter blocking performance. The better vendors acknowledge that no filter can block all proscribed content, and that filters sometimes block Internet sites that according to the company's criteria should not have been blocked. In TIFAP, we found that the single most important feature determining information-retrieval performance was whether keyword blocking could be disabled. Enabled, keyword blocking made testers say "no" one-third of the time to the question, "were you able to find what you were looking for?" With keyword blocking disabled, information retrieval improved significantly—to hit rates of 80 and 90 percent. (The other very important feature was the ability to selectively enable categories, which is discussed in Chapter 5.) However, after keyword blocking was disabled, some filters continued to perform poorly, though in the other direction (letting through sexually-explicit sites, for example, when this category was enabled for blocking in the filter). These filters rely too heavily on keyword blocking, perhaps for the economic factors discussed in Chapter 2, "Types of Filtering Software."

The performance issues related to keyword blocking mean you shouldn't purchase a product unless you know you can disable keyword blocking (which you will verify by testing the product—see Chapter 4, "Planning to Purchase a Filter"). Some products, such as Bess, come configured with keyword blocking capabilities which you can't disable yourself, but which can be disabled on request. Two client products, Cybersitter and Surfwatch, do not allow keyword blocking to be disabled, and they are noted as unacceptable purchases in the product-review section for this reason. (Note that Surfwatch comes in server-based versions which may perform quite differently than did the client version.)

Be warned that most of the companies touting their keyword-blocking ability wrap it in very fancy language, such as "content recognition" or, in the case of URLab's I-Gear, "Dynamic Document Review (DDR).

It seriously strains credulity to think that the most difficult problem in information science has been solved by one company, but some of these vendors ardently and sincerely believe in the value of keyword blocking. The polite thing to do is ensure keyword blocking can be disabled and then test the software. I suspect you will see for yourself, as we saw in TIFAP, and as other libraries have discovered, that even fairly sophisticated keyword blocking, such as I-Gear's, still interferes with information retrieval.

However, as discussed in Chapter 1, "What Filters Are and How They Work," once you disable keyword blocking, no filter can prevent you from accessing sites that its human content selectors don't know about—and you are not guaranteed of getting everywhere you intend to go, either. TIFAP results support the anecdotal evidence reported by libraries that with keyword blocking disabled, between 5 and 15 percent of the "bad stuff" (however you define it) will get through; how much depends on the filter company's reliance on keyword blocking and the thoroughness of the people they hire to identify content to block.

I strongly encourage you to persuade your funding authorities that, based on field experience with filters, you really don't want keyword blocking, and that you'll have to cope with the "bad stuff" some other way.

2D Filter Blocks or Allows to File Level

Blocking to the file level means that a filter can block or enable this file:

http://www.foobird.com/

But still allow or disable this file:

http://www.foobird.com/birds/happy.html

Not all filters can block to the file level. Some only block or enable by domain (e.g. http://www.foobird.com). Even some filters which overall perform well in this regard can run into a perplexing problem if the top site meets blocking criteria and the files under it do not. Bess handled our one good example of this with flying colors, selectively enabling several very good subdirectories on a site where the rest of the site is pornographic; several other filters, including Smart Filter and Websense, blocked the entire site because of the sexual content of the top site. Websense support staff contacted me several times to communicate that they were aware of this problem but did not have a technical fix.

2E Hostnames Resolve to IP Address

There's one more related feature that will affect how well you can block identified sites: the ability to resolve hostnames to IP addresses, and vice versa. Internet addresses such as http://www.census.gov are pseudonyms. Internet computers read addresses as numbers. If you use an Internet tool that can translate this for you,[1] you can see that www.census.gov, the computer that serves the Census bureau, is represented by the numbers, 148.129.129.31. This is the literal IP (Internet Protocol) address for that particular resource. Computers use a service called DNS, the Domain Naming System, to translate the IP address into a form humans can remember. (The IP address is sometimes called "dotted quad," since its numbers always fall across four segments separated by three periods.)

A good feature for a filter, then, is to be able to know that http://www.census.gov is the same as http://148.129.129.31. Otherwise you could block http://www.census.gov, but anyone with a little technical knowledge (or even just a list of IP addresses) could type in http://148.129.129.31. (Try it yourself without a filter. Note that the numbers might change, which is another reason why the naming system exists.)

Not all filters include the ability to resolve hostnames to IP addresses. How important this feature is depends on how determined you are to prevent folks from deliberately accessing Internet resources you want to block. Only infrequently will anyone "accidentally" display Websites accessible by IP addresses, since most Websites are known by their alphabetical addresses. If the reason you're using a filter is because of concern over what people will stumble across, versus what they will deliberately seek out, this feature should be a low priority for you.

3. SITE LISTS

3A Extensive Site List

The reason you are using a filter is to prevent access (or warn prior to access) to sites on the Internet. With keyword blocking disabled, the site list, then, becomes extremely important (though see Chapter 5, "Web Rating Systems," for a discussion of PICS and its potential impact on what is selected). You want an extensive site list—and you want it to be extensive in the areas you want to block.

Ask how many people maintain the site list. As mentioned elsewhere in this book, these site lists are labor-intensive to create and maintain. The fewer people who are dedicated to this task, the shorter and less accurate the list will be. You may not be able to get a vendor to answer this question—which is revealing in itself!

The size of the site list is important, but it is also an easy figure to distort. If you have ever followed discussions about how big a search engine's database is, you know there are many ways to count the same data. Is every file counted? Every individual graphic? Every Website? Every site ever added, or just the current list?

While you want this information, take it with an exceptionally large grain of salt. You will know how useful the site list is when you test the filter. Obviously, "thousands" is lower than "hundreds of thousands"; beyond that, the proof will be in the pudding.

A very large site list may still be inadequate if it doesn't include enough of the sites you're targeting. If you know that you only want to block a very specific area—if, for example, like many librarians, you want to block only pornography-related sites—take note that most of the filter vendors spread themselves very thinly across many categories of sites. Filters with many categories performed well in TIFAP, but we were focusing on sexually-explicit information. You are, of course, paying for the entire site list, regardless of how little of it you use. Again, the proof is in the pudding: test that filter.

3B List of Blocked Sites Is Viewable

Only two products evaluated, Net Nanny and The Library Channel, actually let someone with administrative privileges view the blocked sites. Because of this, I wanted to really like these products, but they both have major problems that need to be resolved (see the product reviews). Furthermore, most companies aren't planning to let you view their site lists—at least not for a while.

Why is viewing site lists such an issue? The twin issues are freedom of information and accountability. In theory, if the filter always worked as advertised, we could trust the companies to select information according to the filter categories and not worry about what they were selecting. But classifying information—as librarians know all too well—is a very subjective area. Even with standard subject headings, two librarians will often disagree on how to classify a new book. Filter companies have attempted to classify information (at least the kind of information they think people want to block), but they haven't applied any industry-wide standards as we have in librarianship for traditional paper-based media (books, for example).

We know, not only through TIFAP but also anecdotally, that filters do not work well all the time. This should not surprise you. Nothing works well all the time; that's why cars have oil lights and houses have fuseboxes. Sometimes human error happens, and a site is inappropriately classified. Sometimes the filter vendor's "philosophy" isn't congruent with yours.

You may have very different ideas of what is "gross," "unacceptable," "pornographic" and so forth. (In TIFAP, the most important factor determining how a site was rated was who was rating it.) Sometimes filter companies use their blocking ability to promote their agenda; Cybersitter blocks a Website critical of its product[2]. The potential is always there, and if the filter's site list is a digital "closed stack," how will you know? Checks and balances are part of many situations in life involving confidence and trust—without them, we are in the uneasy position of being forced to hope for the best. Examples of these checks and balances include bank statements, community property laws, and the branches of the federal government.

Keeping site lists private is, on the other hand, understandable from the vendor's perspective. This is a market decision about a labor-intensive commodity, and as someone who has run a business, I do understand that high-value company secrets need to be closely guarded. I don't fault vendors on this. They aren't forcing anyone to buy their product. But I do think the library community needs more discussion on this topic.

3C List of Blocked Sites Is Editable

Since you can't view the site list on most filters, it follows that you can't edit it, either. If a vendor says this is possible, ask specifically if he or she means that you can create secondary access or denial lists—that's probably what the vendor means. Net Nanny is the only product so far that really allows you to edit the site list, except for The Library Channel (which is built around locally-defined access lists).

3D Supports Local Access/Deny Lists

Local access/deny lists hold sites that the users identify for inclusion or exclusion by the filter. These sites represent errors, or differences of opinion, with respect to the master site list provided by the vendor.

Because no single site list can apply to all settings, an important question is how long this list can be. The client version of Cyber Patrol, up through version 4.0, evaluated just before this book went to press, only holds 64 URLs. That's not very much; if you put one URL in the list every week, it would fill up in a year. This feature was due to change. Ask first, because that list isn't good enough.

A good feature in local access/deny lists is to be able to categorize their URLs. This really only becomes important if your list gets very long, but the section 5E, which discusses local holdings, explains why you are better off, in many cases, adding to a local access/deny list than requesting site additions and deletions from the vendor's master list.

3E Supports Shared Lists
3F Supports Third-Party Lists
3G Supports Customized Lists

Shareable lists is an interesting feature found in one product, The Library Channel, and mentioned to me as a possible enhancement for future versions of several other products. In theory, you could swap, share, merge and otherwise share combined site lists. Read Chapter 7, though, for a discussion of what's wrong with master lists in the first place.

I asked vendors about support for third-party and customized lists because of my street sense, bolstered by TIFAP findings, that most libraries are primarily interested in blocking pornography, though occasionally are interested in controlling resources such as Internet Relay Chat and telnet from a resource-allocation perspective. Vendors were often cautious about using a third-party list—less, I think, because of the sense of ownership they have for their own data than due to the sheer labor involved in adapting such a list to their system. However, they also indicated that they were open to discussion and, being vendors, were receptive to what the market wanted.

Leave open the possibility that a third-party service will come along offering a customized site list that works with your filter's technology. (It may even be a labeling bureau, if the PICS technology, discussed in Chapter 5 catches on.) If your vendor's database is organized by an open standard, this will be easier to accomplish. Meanwhile, the simplest example of this feature—which is a potential feature, not something you can use now—would be if a third-party came out with a site list that blocked only those sites you found objectionable, and which the filter vendor you work with supports.

The filter you look at, or decide to purchase, may not offer support for third-party lists, but you should keep this kind of option in mind when you negotiate the license.

3H Site List Updated Automatically
3I Site List Maintained Daily

Most server-based filters, and even some client filters, offer automatic updates, so you can schedule updating the filter's site list. That's one less chore for you. This feature is only useful if you have a dedicated connection, but it is a timesaver.

New Websites show up every day, and some vendors provide daily incremental updates. A few update by the week, and a couple update less frequently.

4. BLOCKING BY TIME/PLACE/MANNER

4A Block by Protocol
4B Block by Time
4C Supports Time-Outs

We tend to think of "the Web," but there are other tools on the Internet besides the Web. These other protocols are identified in URLs by their different prefixes, as in telnet, irc, news, ftp, and mailto. Folks who have been on the Internet for a long time remember when each resource had to be launched by a separate tool; these days the Web is rapidly (but not completely) integrating most of these activities under the http (Web protocol) umbrella.

Particularly in terms of using a filter for resource allocation, the ability to block a protocol entirely is very useful, more so when it can be used in conjunction with time blocking. With both protocol and time blocking, if your computers are consistently tied up from 3–6 p.m. every day by kids using chat groups and playing MUDs (interactive games on the Internet), you could combine blocking of irc and telnet, and enable category blocking of chat groups, as well. (Chat groups are sometimes Web based, and thus not easily separated out by protocol—you definitely don't want to block http!). You might then end up enabling a number of groups selectively for these periods—but if you have a feedback tool and have good reporting features, you'll have good information on which to base your decision.

After talking to libraries and vendors, there's one feature not available as of this writing I think we can expect to see very shortly in at least some products: session time-outs. In a session time-out, a user might have, for example, thirty minutes with a service; the computer would then time out. (Libraries often offer time-outs through manual sign-up sheets, and some libraries use separate software just for this purpose.) A nice feature with time-outs is a prompt for time-out after periods of inactivity. A good variation on time-outs would be time-outs through patron or workstation authentication (with administrative override, so a librarian working with a patron wouldn't see the search vanish off the screen). Combined with protocol blocking, this could, for example, let a library establish one set of limits for chat and another for general research or use of OPAC.

4D Multiple Configuration Options
4E Access by Barcode

At their simplest, some client-based filters allow one level of access with password override for accessing blocked sites. However, unless you are a very small library, you're looking for more.

Providing better control over "who has access to what, and where" is a fairly high priority for most libraries interested in filters. One area you should examine closely when looking at a filter is how well it can support the different levels of access you currently have in the library, both for content and for computer security. Even if everyone can check out anything, at any time, look around—because you do have some levels of access. Interlibrary loan and circulation information are two types of data we guard closely, and we do not let patrons check out reference books, reconfigure our computers or log in to the administrator's module for a look inside the various modules of our online catalog. The reasons for access levels vary from social attitudes about what children see, to fiscal control, to the need for a secure computer system.

TIFAP testing indicated that some testers wanted to be more stringent with children than with adults. This isn't too surprising when you consider that many library systems require children to get parental permission to access adult material. Often this access is controlled through information stored in the library patron database, where every patron record is associated with a barcode.

For that matter, librarians often have access to resources that the public does not, such as variable-rate databases or fileservers where library data is stored, and an even smaller handful of staff usually have the keys to the automated kingdom (and they have the gray hair to prove it).

Similarly, for a filter, you may want to have several levels of staff access: for the people who maintain the system, for the people who add and delete sites from the system, and for the staff "on the front line" who need the ability to override features. The least expensive client-based filters lump together administrative control with password override of blocked sites. The server-based tools and one client, The Library Channel, were much more robust in this respect. I-Gear offered particularly powerful fine-tuning of access levels.

There are two popular methods for controlling user access in libraries: controlling computers by location (usually associated with the IP, or Internet, address of the computer), or controlling access by user authorization—such as adult versus child. So there could be a group of computers associated with the children's room, and these computers could have one level of access; or the computers could be anywhere in the library, but access is controlled by patron login. Ideally, both capabilities are available.

Flexibility in configuration is a rapid growth area for these products, since the filter companies have realized that libraries have much different needs than the other markets these companies have worked with so far. In the summer of 1997, some filter vendors were offering by-workstation configuration in some versions of their products, with greater capabilities projected shortly. I-Gear offers very powerful configuration in this respect, allowing you to create different groups of clients (computers) and users, with precise access levels. This would mean that you could have different blocking for every computer in your library—or, more logically, that certain computers in some areas, and/or some users in some groups, would have different levels of access.

Still more interesting is the frontier of user authentication, which is new turf for most filter vendors, in part because most of their growth area so far has been in the business or school arenas, where people spend all day behind one computer. The very different library environment, where computer users are nomadic and transitory, are linked to patron data held in a barcode, and do not "belong" to the computer they are using except for the duration of their session, is a new—but not unwelcome—concept to filter vendors.

With the potential of user-based access comes the potential of remote authentication—perhaps not only to restrict access, but also to authorize it for licensed databases, or to "tune" the first access point to files customized for special user groups (such as children, visually disabled patrons, older users, or other special groups). But this is simply my own speculation—I like to piggyback as much technology as possible on one purchase.

4F Filter Supports Warn vs. Block

Some library systems have expressed an interest in a warn vs. block feature—that is, instead of blocking sites, they are considering presenting a warning message that notifies the patron that the targeted links were identified as, for example, pornographic. In conjunction with patron authentication, this feature could be used to block some sites in the children's room while providing potential access to these sites for adult patrons and library staff who choose to follow these links.

While only one (client-based) filter I assessed currently offered warn vs. block, all vendors for server-based software said this would not be difficult to implement if there were a demand for it. That makes sense, since most filters currently have some override feature at present. Several vendors plan to add this feature shortly.

5. FILTER CATEGORIES

5A Site List Arranged in Categories
5B Categories Can Be Selectively Enabled

Most filters have categories, and most filters allow you to enable or disable categories. Libraries primarily concerned with blocking pornography need both features because you need to disable most of the categories for filters to be usable in an information-retrieval environment. Filter categories are arbitrary and capricious to begin with, and the farther the filter category strays from the truly pornographic sites, the less likely it is that these tools will reflect these categories, however carefully they are described in any manual.

Whether a filter has ten or thirty categories is not as important as whether you can precisely define what it is you do or do not want patrons to access. However, it is worth asking whether a company that is distributing content selection across 30 general categories is going to be robust or even precise in an area you select. This was a question with Websense, which has 28 categories, ranging from "Activist groups" to "Entertainment." Our TIFAP tester found that the Websense categories seemed precise in the areas of pornography but somewhat careless in chat, with about half of the chat sites available through a casual Yahoo search accessible. Overall, with filters, some of the blocking in areas not related to sexuality seems desultory.

Values of the people identifying and classifying sites to block became readily apparent in TIFAP testing. Several filters blocked a variety of AIDS and safe-sex information under categories such as "adult" or "Sexuality/Lifestyle," prompting queries to filter vendors that were not always satisfactorily answered. Several of the TIFAP testers suggested a range of granularity for sexually-oriented material to allow customers to fine-tune their site selections.

Remember that filter categories are extremely arbitrary, and are often designed, as several vendors emphasized to me, with multiple markets in mind—businesses and home use, as well as libraries. I personally feel very uneasy about doing business with a company that sells people the ability to block information I feel everyone should have access to. Here you will have to let your circumstances be your guide. Be sure to familiarize yourself with the various categories, and ask vendors *exactly* what they mean by phrases such as "adult," "controversial," "nudity," or "alternative lifestyle." Because you can't view the site lists, you will really only understand what is in the categories by selectively enabling and disabling these categories. This is another reason to test any filter you plan to use in a library.

5C Filter Supports Library-Defined Categories

You may want to create local categories for several reasons. For example, if your local access/deny lists become long, you will want to categorize them. In theory, you could even collect Websites in a particular area to highlight for access—temporarily deny access to all other categories and let a patron do a very focused search for jobhunting resources, for example.

5D Categories Correspond with LCSH

Some filters allow you to define additional categories. No filter organizes categories by Library of Congress Subject Headings. I wouldn't really expect this, though LCSH is an international standard. I raise this primarily to emphasize, again, that filter categories are idiosyncratic and unique to each vendor.

5E Local Holdings

When, in the course of this book, I talked to filter vendors, a couple of times I asked questions that only a librarian would think up. The biggest question I had—and it came from observing filter performance over a few months—is how they handle the issue of one central database defining all local access. In my mind I saw a different library, every day, requesting a site be added...blocked... added... blocked, and in some cases I think I actually saw this happen, even with TIFAP's very limited URL set.

We know each community is unique; that's what makes libraries so wonderful—because we are so attuned to our communities. But that uniqueness also makes central databases problematical. To librarians, there is an obvious reverse analogy. Think of OCLC. It's an international bibliographic database with master records tagged with local holdings. When you create a local online catalog for the first time, you download the records associated with your holdings. When your branch libraries add or subtract items, the local catalog becomes further refined, reflecting each site's holdings.

Compared to this, the bibliographic organization of filters is extremely crude. Imagine that OCLC's master database had no holdings, and you only had a rough list of exceptions to the list to determine what your local catalog looked like. This is the best you can do with respect to local customization of the filter master database.

I will say that every vendor I have spoken to was intrigued by this discussion, and was interested in OCLC and how it was organized. I do believe there are solutions, and it is remotely possible that these solutions are related to the Web rating schemes currently under discussion. But it's essential, first, to recognize that a central database that cannot be tagged for local holdings is a problem from the start.

Meanwhile, it's vital that you have robust local access/deny lists, and it will help if you can assign the access/deny resources to categories so you can better manage them. In Websense, for example, if you had chat disabled but wanted to allow one of the very good chat groups for cancer survivors, you could add the chat group to your local access list, and be sure that you would always have access to it. You would also be able to categorize it as a chat group. That's the kind of careful organization we librarians are known for, and there is no reason not to implement and refine these skills in the online environment.

6. OTHER FEATURES TO LOOK FOR

6A Recommend Changes to Master List

Nearly all filters provide methods for recommending the addition or deletion of sites from the vendor's master list. Sometimes this input feature is built very smoothly into the system. The default "blocked" pages for Bess and I-Gear provide links to the vendor's email, for example. Other filters, such as Cyber Patrol, provide reconsideration tools built into the filter which are limited to users with administrative access. None of the tools provided for automated tracking of the reconsideration request and the company's decision.

6B Strong User Diagnostics and Feedback

User diagnostics and feedback tools are two of the most significant features in filters.

By user diagnostics, I mean what information the filter provides when a site is blocked. Some filters do not provide any feedback beyond stopping information in transit or obliterating words in context. Others provide a very brief message, such as "Cyber Patrol Code 2." This is meaningful only if you (or your patrons) know what "Code 2" is. Surfwatch provided the cryptic message, "Blocked by Surfwatch" (Why? How? What are my options?), while Cybersitter provided no information whatsoever. Note that different versions of the same product may be different in this capability. Cyber Patrol's client does not offer an editable blocking message, but its LAN and proxy-server versions do. Most server-based filters I looked at offered messages that can be customized by the library, and those that did not, such as I-Gear, planned to in the near future.

A good, basic default message is helpful for designing a good denial page. Bess has a very clear default message that includes a link to suggest adding the site and a place for the person with override authorization to quickly input a password. Smart Filter, additionally, informs the end user which category the offending URL falls into. This last feature is particularly helpful for determining if the block represents a philosophical decision (as in, this filter company believes this information is inappropriate under any circumstances because it promotes drug use) or human error (the filter company placed this Website into the wrong category).

No filter as of this writing provided different messages for different settings, though again, vendors said this feature could be implemented if enough people asked for it, and several products may offer support for multiple denial pages by the time this book is published. Libraries serving different age groups, different languages, or different areas (such as a branch of a large library) could benefit from this feature.

Regarding feedback, some filters provide email links to the vendors. I recommend bringing the library into the feedback loop. If your computer department can support it, and the filter you're looking at doesn't offer this capability, consider creating a "suggestion box" form that directs mail to both you and the vendor. You can use this form to monitor the vendor's response and/or evaluate the site for potentially adding or deleting from local site lists.

6C PICS Support

Much ballyhooed, but yet unrealized, this is the scheme to rate the entire Internet using technology enabled by the Platform for Internet Content Selection (PICS), the subject of Chapter 5. Not one vendor saw PICS happening overnight (and neither do I), but on the outside chance that this feature might become real, and because it is a "marketing check-off," most filter vendors have either enabled their software for PICS support or plan to do so in the near future.

6D Patron Notice Cannot Be Disabled

Based on what I have seen with filter performance, I believe we should not have the ability to disable a notification message. In other words, a filter should not silently redirect to another page when it blocks a site. Patrons are entitled to know what we are doing on their behalf. I doubt that software engineers will write the capability to disable notification out of their products, since it is in demand (one TIFAP tester used a server-based product with silent redirects, since this is how the library had configured it). However, we can at least ask our colleagues to provide patron notices that inform users why the information was blocked and what they can do if they disagree with the block.

SUMMARY: PUTTING FILTER FEATURES TO USE

You have some options here. You can use these features to negotiate with a vendor for the product you really want. Take these features to a trustees meeting, or to a community group, to discuss what filters can and cannot do. Go on a radio talk show and explain how filters really work, and how to distinguish among them. Launch your own study of filters, and come up with solutions. Have staff meetings where you discuss Internet content and how filters do and do not address it.

For those of you who are seriously considering use of a filter, understanding filter features should empower you to tell—not ask—companies what you expect from a product (whether or not they can deliver these features). I have worked with some very good vendors while writing this book, but I still feel compelled to tell you: the customer is always right. You are the customer. You are right! If a product doesn't look right, feel right, or smell right, and the vendor can't make it better on your schedule, don't use it. Tell the vendor why you don't like it, and press on.

In the next chapter, I explain how to go about purchasing a filter.

NOTES

1. If you have access to a Unix account, the *host* command can do this; for example, at the Unix prompt, try:

   host http://www.census.gov

   This command should return the IP address, if the host program is working.
2. Specifically, the teen-run Peacefire Website, at http://www.peacefire.org

4

Planning to Purchase a Filter

So you are planning to purchase a filter? Go into this project understanding that a filter is not a single solution, that you are adding additional expense and labor to your annual budget, and that in a year or less this purchase decision may well be OBE (Overcome By Events). Things change so fast in the online environment that this year's solution is next year's unwanted baggage.

Still, sometimes it may seem that a filter is the best solution—and if you're going to make a decision, make the best one you can.

TEST THAT FILTER!

Starting with the next section of this chapter, I'll walk you through planning a product selection cycle for filters. But one component of that cycle needs to be discussed up front.

If you are seriously considering using a filter in your library, I have three crucial pieces of advice for you:

1. *Test the product*
2. *Test the product*
3. *Test the product*

If you don't test the product, it doesn't matter how carefully you plan and implement the rest of your product decisions, because you won't know what you are buying. If we learned anything through TIFAP, it is that filters behaved better and worse, and most importantly, *differently* than what we expected. Most vendors expect you to test the product, anyway; although some companies are just out to make a quick buck, quite a few more are interested in a happy customer, because happy customers breed *more* happy customers.

Now I have another important piece of advice—perhaps the most important lesson from TIFAP. It applies primarily to client-based software:

1. *Don't test the product on a computer you can't afford to be without, even briefly*

Try very hard not to test software on the reference-desk computer. TIFAP testers learned this the hard way, when client software rewrote critical system files, froze the computer, disabled Internet access, and in at least one case required reinstallation of the operating system. All computers were eventually restored to their former working condition, but the time lost for a badly-needed workstation was significant. If you are testing a product which does not actually require installation on your computer, such as access to a remote proxy server like Bess, you can relax this rule. And in some cases, you may only have one computer you can test the product on (in which case, may the force be with you). I'd still strongly advise that experiments with interesting new products, even high-quality server-based products, not happen the day before a visit from the state librarian or on the eve of debuting Internet access at your library.

YOUR PRODUCT SELECTION CYCLE

Quite frankly, if you have ever evaluated software for your library system, you know as much as you need to about evaluating new products. However, the "smut on the Internet" issue is so hot that it adds additional problems to the software purchasing cycle. At least ten times during the course of TIFAP, I was contacted by a librarian for assistance because a community group was pressuring the local government to make the library use a particular software tool. Imagine if you were trying to select your next online catalog or system-wide word-processing program while concerned citizens monitored your every move and pushed you to choose a product they'd read about in the newspaper or found surfing Yahoo!

Whether or not you are under pressure, it behooves you to build

Software Selection Cycle Timeframe (Sample)

Week 1: Identify Operating Environment	Talk to computer folks, walk through library, make list, coordinate your notes with computer folks.
Week 2: Decide What You Want the Filter to Do	Decide *why* you are buying a filter so you know *what* to buy.
Week 3: Identify Current Products	Re-read this book, review Websites, post questions to discussion lists.
Week 4: Contact Potential Vendors	Email and call vendors to ask about trials.
Week 5: Design Filter Tests	Meet with staff to discuss potential purchase, then designate project honchos and assign taskings.
Weeks 6 and 7: Test Filters	Make sure this is going on when folks are actually around to test these tools; document your results.
Weeks 8 and 9: Make Decision	Meet with your decision-makers; wheel and deal with vendors.
Week 10: Begin Deployment	Try to avoid doing this during Banned Books Week.

a very clear-cut and intentional software selection cycle, and stick to your timeframe even if you have to back-burner or delegate everything else that needs getting done. (I promise you will be very, very tired of filters by the end of this project.) After you build your timeframe, let concerned parties know what your schedule is. Remember to build a testing period into your timeframe. If you have a month or two, that's not ideal, but it's better than nothing. See the sample timeframe below. It's a very linear design—you will probably do several of these steps simultaneously—but like the filter testing schedule (which itself is a subset of this plan), it provides a visible and tidy structure to your actions, like lining up ingredients on the kitchen counter before you bake a cake.

WEEK 1: IDENTIFYING YOUR NETWORK OPERATING ENVIRONMENT

"Identifying your network operating environment" is just fancy lingo for determining what you can use and what you can live with. The common-sense rule here is that whatever you eventually purchase has to work with your existing software and hardware (and not annoy the heck out of the folks who maintain the computers). You have some decision-making information from the chapter on filter features, and vendors will have a lot of preliminary information you can use to rule out some products and identify potential candidates. You will also be doing a lot of snooping, as I cover below in Week 2, but keep in mind that you won't really know how the tool works in your environment until you test it.

Your computer support staff need to be involved in the selection process, and now is the time to bring them in. They are best able to advise you on the limits of your network operating system, and will need to evaluate the product you are considering as a potential member of the family of software you currently use.

WEEK 2: THE NEEDS ASSESSMENT: DECIDE WHAT YOU WANT THE FILTER TO DO

Needs assessment is crucial—don't even think of skipping this step. It's one thing to know how filters work; it's another altogether to revisit why you decided to investigate using filters in the first place. The confluence of the two will ultimately determine what you select.

As pointed out in the previous chapter, context is everything. If the pressure-point is one computer located in the children's room, implementing an expensive network-wide system would be overkill. If your Internet computers aren't on a local area network, you will have to use client software anyway, unless you decide to use a remote proxy server or filter through an ISP (see Chapter 2, "Types of Filtering Software," for more discussion about these types of filters.) If, on the other hand, you believe you will need a network-wide solution you definitely don't want to select a filter that requires extensive fiddling with each and every computer in the system.

Needs Brainstorming Checklist

Worried about sexually-explicit material at kids' computers

Chat heavy at peak hours—hard to control

Frank and Susan need to monitor from home

Want good reports, so we can base decisions on facts

Don't make work for tech support!

Needs Brainstorming

Pull your staff together and brainstorm about the top issues you think a filter should address. If this is a tough issue for people to discuss publicly, have them cast ballots first. This is much preferable to shouting matches about what is or what is not appropriate in a library setting.

Look at Server-based solutions if you . . .	Look at Client-based solutions if you . . .
Have a local area network	Do not have local area network
Plan to use filter on all or most computers	Plan to use filter on a small percentage of computers
Have many computers	Have a few computers
Have your own Internet domain	Do not have your own domain
Have in-house network support	Do not have in-house network support
Need central control of the filter	Can distribute control of the filter
And look at remote proxy servers if you have few computers and/or limited technical support	

Maybe the Answer Isn't a Filter

After you develop your needs assessment, try to identify solutions that are not based on using filters. It's possible that a filter is the wrong solution for the problem, or you only need a handful of features some of these filters offer. I have been contacted by librarians who only wanted to prevent patrons from logging in to chat groups during peak hours of use of the library catalog. Some filters don't support time/place/manner blocking, and some aren't specific enough to block chat, and only chat. Some of the more expensive products did not, as of this writing, block Usenet, a major component of chat.

If you're looking for controlling computer sessions, there are software programs that time-out sessions at preset intervals, and some libraries get by quite well with sign-up sheets or even, in some relaxed environments, signs that say "20 minute limit at computers when others are waiting." Other libraries may decide to use filters set only to blocking chat for designated periods during the day. I-Gear is one filter that has built in extensive time management. Other libraries might use a monitoring program such as On Guard or Cyber Snoop to determine if they have a problem with chat abuse in the first place.

There are more ideas for procedures and tools to use in place of, or with, filters in Chapter 6, "Advice from the Trenches," which includes real-life examples and product information.

WEEK 3: IDENTIFY CURRENT PRODUCTS

First you need to know what's out there. See the website for this book for current lists of filters. But don't stop there! Visit related links, search the big search engines (like Alta Vista), and ask questions on library-related discussion lists. Don't be surprised if your post to a discussion list is met with a deafening silence, at least publicly. Many folks feel uncomfortable discussing their decision to use filters.

It's also time to start getting the real story on how these products work. Get it from the horse's mouth. Ask the vendor for references for people who actually purchased this product. Don't just take the vendor's word for it—follow up on the contacts and talk to them personally about their experiences. If you don't get concrete information, keep calling around and sending email until you find someone who will give you the low-down. No product works perfectly, and anyone who has only praise for a software package isn't the person to whom you need to be speaking. When the person you call asks you, "What do you want first—the good news or the bad news?" you know you've found a good source.

Don't be too discouraged if, after you factor in your network operating environment and the features that are "bottom line" for you, your working list of potential filters has only two or three products on it. There seems to be a subset of Murphy's Law that says you will never have more than three products to choose from, regardless of how many brands exist.

WEEK 4: CONTACT POTENTIAL VENDORS

Now is the time to approach the vendors whose products interest you. If nobody taught you this mantra in library school, learn it here: "Vendors Are Your Friends." They may not always be your best or most trustworthy friends, but they nearly always are invaluable allies in your search for the product you want. Even if you rule out a product early on in the testing because it doesn't work out correctly, if you have been on good terms with that vendor, the information you provide will probably find its way back to the folks who maintain the software—which is good for everyone. And if you develop a longer relationship with that vendor—down to "walking down the aisle" with a product purchase—your input *will* change

---

Additional Resources for Locating Filters

Library-Oriented Lists and Serials
http://info.lib.uh.edu/liblists/liblists.htm
Database for locating library-related discussion groups

Practical Guide to Filters
http://www.bluehighways.com/filters/
Website for this book; includes updated product information

Filteringfacts
http://www.filteringfacts.org
A nonprofit organization devoted to championing filters in libraries. Includes articles and pointers to information about filters.

Yahoo
http://www.yahoo.com
Has a good basic list that can be found by using keywords *filtering* and *blocking*

---

that product in the long run. This is particularly true in new fields, such as filters, where vendors seem eager to get input from their potential customer base.

Once you get a sales rep assigned to you, contact that person regularly to touch base. If there is something you really like about the product, particularly a new feature, or if the sales rep did something nice, say so. Email is a great medium because vendors can forward messages to other departments; not too long ago I sent praise to a vendor who wrote me back the same day to say, "You just made a lot of people happy."

By the way, this may be obvious to some of you old hands, but I learned through experience not to contact a vendor unless the product had the potential to meet my minimum requirements for the time of purchase. Most vendors are good at what they do, and will not leave you alone until they are absolutely certain you are "not a sale." If you absolutely know you can't use a product, however interesting any one feature, don't talk to a vendor about it.

One of the first topics you should open discussion on is the price.

What are you getting for your money?

I know I use the term "buy a filter" very loosely in this book. In many cases what you will actually do is license a product or service for a set period. The nature of this agreement is something you should examine very carefully, particularly with something like filter software. If you are paying thousands of dollars to license a product, you're entitled to ask some tough questions such as:

- Can you get a 30–day money-back guarantee?
- What are the limits of that guarantee?
- Are you licensing a version or a time period?
- Are you eligible for all product upgrades during the license period?

If this is new ground for you, I particularly recommend you read the following article, which includes sensible advice for all kinds of electronic licenses and purchases: Wilson, Thomas C. "Zen and the Art of CD-ROM Network License Negotiation." *The Public-Access Computer Systems Review 1*, no. 2 (1990): 4 - 14. Online at: http://info.lib.uh.edu/pr/v1/n2/wilson.1n2

Additionally, you will want your filter to do two things: perform correctly, and block targeted information. To do this, you will need both technical support and current site lists. Not all vendors include these in the "base" price.

Site Licensing

Unless you are definitely going to buy client software, you are going to have to negotiate a site license. A good time to do this with any software is when a new version comes out and the product is available at special prices to entice new customers (like you). Consider no price firm unless you are constitutionally incapable of bargaining. If you currently use another product and are looking for new products, don't appear too enthusiastic about anything you're looking at, no matter how much you hate your current product; you want to be in a position to get a break in the price.

Generally, filters that are licensed on a site basis are priced either "per workstation" or "per simultaneous user." Buyers for very large networks (Wide Area Networks or Metropolitan Area Networks) are old hats at the (long, agonizing) site licensing process, which probably has scads of rules and guidelines to keep you busy on this project for a while, and you don't need advice from me. Librarians with smaller networks that include branches should remember that vendors unfamiliar with library settings may need to be educated on the network topology of libraries, with our central and branch libraries. The idea here is to persuade the vendors, as much as possible, that branches are not so much separate entities as little chips off the old block, so that they don't get over-enthusiastic with site licensing. Don't underestimate the role of the salesperson in making this call. I price databases for a 4–part geographic region spanning state lines and even an ocean, and when my sales representatives change, so does my pricing, every time.

Pricing Filters: Elementary Questions

Base software price for your site
Including all users and workstations

List subscription price, if separate
Length of subscription and frequency of update are key

Technical support
How many hours a week, response time, who can call in questions, and how long the period of support is for; and is this an extra purchase or included in the price?

Warranty
What it covers, how long it is for, what if you have persistent problems that cause you to remove the program

---

WEEKS 5, 6 AND 7: DESIGN THE TEST, AND TEST THAT FILTER!

By testing the product, I mean a) installing a full-featured (not "demo") version of the product in the environment you plan to use it in, and b) spending as much time as you can afford examining how well this filter performs in a real-world setting, using end-users and public-access librarians. You also need to have your computer gurus walk these tools through their paces (and they may nix the product early on, if it conflicts with other automated services or turns out to be missing major features). However, your computer gurus can't substitute for end-users or reference librarians, because they spend too much time away from public service and know too much about the software they install and maintain. But you can't rely on reference librarians, either; librarians are skilled at circumventing information problems, and even when we want to, we can't disable our skills. (We acknowledged this trait in TIFAP.) You want to know how these filters perform when people don't understand how they work and aren't competent searchers.

Yes, testing filters will add time—a lot of it—to your product selection cycle, and you need to plan carefully, because if the product doesn't perform well, you then have to test another one (unless you are able to have concurrent tests running elsewhere in your library). However, there are five very strong reasons why you should always test a filter before using it in a library setting. These are addressed in the table on the next page.

Guidelines and Honchos

If you've ever designed or managed a project like this, you know your best tool is at least one eager staff person who knows how to "make it happen" and can honcho this program through on schedule. You do need to manage this project closely, however, so make sure it's someone who can and will keep you truly informed.

It's important that decisions about how the filter is configured are not made exclusively by your automation department. Ensure your computer staff and your librarians communicate about the capabilities of the filter and how to handle problems. Topics of discussion should include what can and cannot be disabled, what categories are available and how the company defines them, what librarians and users can expect to see when the software blocks a site, how to handle a site that staff feel is blocked incorrectly, what to do if there are software problems the librarian suspects are related to the filter, monitoring the company's response time with respect to reconsiderations, and upchanneling user comments and questions.

This evaluation period is also a strategic time to discuss reporting capabilities and patron privacy. On the one hand, strong reporting capabilities in an Internet content filter can provide important information about what the filter is blocking and enabling so we know how it actually performs. On the other hand, like all patron information—for example, circulation history and interlibrary loan requests—patron search results are entitled to confidentiality. It is not too early to decide who can see these reports, how long reports are maintained, where they are kept, and what to do if an agency requests them.

Reasons for Testing Filters

1. As TIFAP and every other filter product evaluation have demonstrated, performance issues range wildly across filters.

2. Filter software is evolving rapidly; you can't count on last month's technology being next month's solution.

3. Filter testing is classic librarianship. We've always looked carefully at information services. There's no reason to stop now.

4. Filter testing could have a calming effect on the lynch-mob mentality that sometimes prevails when a precipitating incident creates local concern about "bad stuff on the Internet." A respite from high-pressure tactics could give you time to develop more options and alternatives.

5. No matter what anyone tells you about how filters perform, as TIFAP demonstrated, the assessment is very subjective. Your idea of "bad stuff" is unique to you (as you will discover when you actually begin testing, and discover that everyone *else* has a different idea of what's "bad").

Engage as many staff as possible in implementing the filter. Areas where the reference staff can be particularly helpful include designing the blocking message and identifying which categories to begin with. While you're doing this, if the filter has a monitoring capability, as Websense does, just monitor traffic on your network for several days and have daily staff huddles to assess the results.

Next, have the reference staff test the filters. This will also make it much easier for them to help patrons using computers that have filters installed. The questions we used in TIFAP are in an appendix in the back of this book; you could select several from every category to begin with, or use them as a launchpad for developing your own.

Which settings should you test filters at? I'd suggest you first look at how the filter works at "full throttle." Then peel down the settings to what you think you really want to disable. That's a very conservative approach, so you may end up, as time permits, taking an educated guess, "tweaking" the filter, then and "tweaking" again, based on your results. Chapter 6, "Advice from the Trenches," includes an example of disabling most settings in Cyber Patrol so it primarily blocks sexually-explicit material.

The test period is also a good time to set up administrative accounts and override passwords, if the filter supports these features. In addition to seeing how the filter performs, you also want to interact with it as you will once you have it licensed; for example, if it supports local access/deny lists, begin working with these.

If the filter offers a "warn vs. block" feature, where the patron sees a block and then overrides it, take advantage of it; you can use this feature to identify when the patron chose to override blocks and access information anyway.

This is a great time to look at the reporting capabilities, because if they are good enough you will get very detailed information about what you are doing while you test the filter. While I was assessing I-Gear, for example, I constantly peeked at the reports I was creating in the system. Staff who are new to monitoring status reports may find it fun and exciting to see their searches logged into reports. This is a good time to reintroduce the topic of patron privacy and emphasize that, as with interlibrary loan and circulation records, library staff are obligated to keep this information confidential and refer requests for information to the library administration.

The notification sign and patron survey at the end of this chapter are only examples, intended to get you started. I recommend not putting patrons in the bind of judging what they saw. Simply note what they observed and look at it later. If the filter has good reporting capabilities, you should be able to reconstruct what was going on.

If you have a citizen's group or friend's group that has been inquiring (perhaps pressing) about filters, here is an opportunity to engage them: ask them to assist with exit interviews. You will require additional work to interpret the results, since librarians bring a level of expertise to the information arena not shared by other professions (not that this is generally appreciated). On the other hand, engaging these folks in the hard work of information is a bridge-building exercise that can potentially lead to better understanding of the issues and better communication. If your offer is rebuffed or ignored, file it in your list of nice gestures that didn't work.

WEEKS 8 AND 9: MAKE A DECISION

Will it really take you two weeks to make a decision? Well, it might if you weren't happy with what you found during the filter test. You then have two choices (which are not mutually exclusive): testing another filter, and asking the vendor if the filter can be modified to accommodate your needs. Don't spend good money on vaporware, but if a company says it can support a feature by Day X, and you can wait that long, this is good information.

In some ways, the fact that filter software is new technology is really a benefit to your feature shopping, because vendors are eager to make inroads into the library trade and are just learning what our special needs are. Vendors who have done business primarily with the K-12 or business environments are often surprised by our very different needs, but interested in accommodating what they can. Each potential customer is also a source of information on what makes their product more marketable to the library profession. I have had vendors say "I think we can do this" or even "good idea, we'll implement this" to such important features as patron barcode support, warn-vs.-block, and other features discussed in Chapter 3, "Filter Features," and Chapter 1, "What Filters Are and How They Work."

As you approach your decision, it's time to look very closely at what you're contracting with the company to provide. Take a look at the product review sheet in the back of this book; if one doesn't exist for the particular product you're looking at, look at the template on pages 108–109. Make sure everything you want is covered in the contract.

How do you make a decision about the filter? Go back to your original criteria, and gather together the reports on sites accessed and blocked, the feedback from reference and automation staff, and the feedback from users. Now that you've looked seriously at at least one product, hopefully more, which one stands out? You aren't going to buy a perfect product, but with a piece of software that will cost you money and time and so closely affects information services, you should know where your priorities are.

Look at the Information

What are the tiebreakers? What are the bottom lines? Did the product perform adequately and not interfere with other products? Did the vendor respond promptly to requests for reconsiderations (adding or deleting sites from the master site list)? Were you happy with their decisions? (You will need to request reconsiderations now and then, no matter what the vendor says, since not only do mistakes happen but no one agrees on what—for example—"porn" is. See Chapter 3, "Filter Features," for a longer discussion of problems with a master database.)

In particular, ask, are there any "show-stoppers"? For example, if you want staff to be able to add and delete sites, and that's not available, that's a show-stopper unless the vendor can have it in place by purchase date. If the filter, despite all kinds of "tweaking," still blocked a lot of information you considered appropriate for your library environment—with the understanding that "a lot" could be a few sites for one library, more for another—that too would be a show-stopper. Talk to the vendors to make sure a configuration problem on your end didn't cause the issue.

If this is effective in your library environment, try another straw poll. (In some libraries, staff want input; in other places, staff want to be told what's what. You know your library better than anyone else.)

Don't buy a product with show-stoppers. Look at other products, discuss the problem with your funding authorities, talk to the vendors, but never pay money for something you know you should not purchase.

WEEK 10: DEPLOYMENT

When it comes time to deploy your filter in a public environment, keep in mind that you are making a decision that can be undone, if necessary. If, despite all preliminary testing and tweaking, you realize after deployment that this filter is not a good decision, don't use it. The tool you've selected may be the best tool right now, but remember Scarlett O'Hara's motto: "tomorrow is another day." Keep your eyes open for new solutions, keep an eye on the filter's performance, keep the channels open with the vendors so you know what's coming down the pike, and prepare, as we have prepared so many times in the last several decades, for the next exciting development in librarianship.

Filter Testing Toolkit	
Timetable	Publicizing this schedule may have a calming effect, if emotions are running high on the issue of "bad stuff on the Web." You can also wave it in front of trustees, other funding authorities, and media wanting to know what you're "doing about the bad stuff."
Filter	Arrange with vendor to have full access to the product for the testing period. You want the real McCoy, not a scaled-down version, and you want to be able to configure it as you would use it in your library.
Workstation(s)	If you're planning to use the filter in more than one type of setting, such as adult and child, test the filter on more than one workstation.
Testers	Use mix of public access librarians and end-users, and involve computer folks in assessing technical performance.
Signs (See sample below)	Signs by workstations, or brief half-page pamphlets, can alert patrons that you are testing new software.
Exit Surveys (See sample below)	Using paper forms, web forms, or volunteers with clipboards, to name three cheap methods, find out how the filters affected searching performance.

Attention Internet Users!

We are testing a product called Porn-Be-Gone on this computer. Porn-Be-Gone is designed to block objectionable information. When Porn-Be-Gone retrieves a website that the company has rated objectionable, it displays a warning, then gives you a chance to access the website anyway.

If you run into problems with your Internet search, please contact a librarian immediately, so we can identify and fix the problem.

If you have an extra minute of time, we would be pleased if you would help answer this survey. We are trying to determine if Porn-Be-Gone is a good use of your tax dollars.

Thanks from the staff at The Library!

Sample Library Sign

Exit Survey

Do you have a minute to answer some questions about software we're testing?

What were you looking for?

Did you find what you were looking for?

(yes) (no)

Did you have to override any blocking messages to get to information you needed to answer a question?

(yes) (no)

What else would you like to share with us about your Internet search experience?

Sample Library Survey

5

Web Rating Systems

Many people believe that "filters will soon be a dead issue because PICS will be the new technology." PICS—the Platform for Internet Content Selection—is a technology that enables rating systems based on metadata in Web pages (metadata is discussed below). Software that is PICS-compliant (or soon will be) includes the Microsoft Explorer Web browser and nearly every filtering software evaluated for this book.

PICS, metadata and rating systems have received much more talk than action at this stage, but I have two hunches about PICS. The first is that with the right seed money, PICS will become widespread. The second is that, should PICS become widespread, filtering software will not go away, but will adapt itself to the PICS technology. I am not convinced that PICS will adequately address the issues created either by Internet content or filters. However, I do think that knowing about PICS is important, because (like filters) it is a issue that could creep up on us very quickly.

Some of the topics in this chapter are best understood if you have a working knowledge of HTML, which is beyond the scope of this book. There are many good guides for HTML, but for librarians, my favorite is:

Roy Tennant (1996). *Practical HTML: A Self-Paced Tutorial*. Library Solutions Press.

However, don't be put off by this warning. If you aren't planning to learn HTML any time soon, skip the parts you don't understand and focus on the parts discussing rating systems and software.

WHAT IS METADATA?

Metadata is information about information. OCLC and RLIN records are metadata; these records describe resources (usually, but not always, traditional paper-based resources, such as books). On the Internet, metadata for an Internet resource can be imbedded in the resource or associated with it. There are even developing standards for how this metadata is described, opening the possibility for classifying electronic information with standard language that could be consistently interpreted by a wide variety of tools.

RATING SYSTEMS AND RATING SERVICES

Rating systems provide structured methods for organizations to rate Websites. Rating services are the companies or organizations that assign these ratings (though authors can also rate their own material). In a sense, filter companies have their own rating systems, and function as their own rating services, but as noted earlier, the categories are arbitrary, non-standard, and specific to each company.

There are several rating systems currently available, and anyone, from the ACLU to Family Friendly Libraries, could come up with its own rating system compatible with PICS. Therefore, PICS rating systems, like filtering vendor rating systems, are also arbitrary, non-standard, and specific to each rating company (or organization). However, the rating systems are not tightly integrated into a specific product, but are best thought of as alternative description methods that can be used with any PICS-compliant software. Cyber Patrol, for example, supports two PICS rating systems: RSACI (Recreational Software Advisory Council on the Internet) and SafeSurf. Netshepherd, which has a product review in this book, relies entirely on its own PICS rating system, but the Netshepherd rating system could, in theory, be used by any PICS-compliant tool.

Although PICS rating systems could be designed to describe anything about a resource, from its expiration date to its Library of Congress classification, existing rating systems have categories similar to those found in filters. RSACI, for example, has four main categories: nudity, sex, violence, and language.

The RSACI Website, at http://www.rsac.org, is a good place to learn more about rating systems. You can experiment with assigning RSACI categories to Internet resources through an interactive tool. In rating my library's webpage, I assigned it "0" in each category. In rating the TIFAP webpage, however, I ultimately assigned it a rating of "1" in the language category, since the list of test questions has nonsexual anatomical references used to describe words filters block. I wasn't really sure how to categorize *questions* about sexual activity, and the descriptions of the categories did not help me here.

RSACI Nudity Categories

(n4) frontal nudity that qualifies as a provocative display of nudity
(n3) frontal nudity
(n2) partial nudity
(n1) revealing attire
(n0) none of the above

RSACI Sex Categories

(s4) sex crimes
(s4) explicit sexual acts
(s3) non-explicit sexual acts
(s2) non-explicit sexual touching
(s2) clothed sexual touching
(s1) passionate kissing
(s0) innocent kissing or romance
(s0) none of the above

RSACI Violence Categories

(v4) wanton, gratuitous violence
(v4) extreme blood and gore
(v4) rape
(v3) blood and gore
(v3) intentional aggressive violence
(v3) death to human beings
(v2) the destruction of realistic objects with an implied social presence
(v1) injury to human beings

(v1)   the death of non-human beings resulting from natural acts or accidents
(v1)   damage to or disappearance of realistic objects
(v0)   sports violence
(v0)   none of the above

Language

(l4)   crude, vulgar language
(l4)   explicit sexual references
(l4)   extreme hate speech
(l4)   epithets that advocate violence or harm against a person or group
(l3)   strong language
(l3)   obscene gestures
(l3)   hate speech or strong epithets against any person or group
(l2)   profanity
(l2)   moderate expletives
(l1)   non-sexual anatomical reference
(l1)   mild expletives
(l1)   mild terms for body functions
(l1)   slang
(l0)   none of the above

WHAT HAPPENS NEXT?

When you submit a RSACI form, RSACI uses this information to create a metadata label for the site. (Entire directories, subdirectories and individual files can be rated.) These labels are temporarily displayed after you submit the form and are also emailed to the point of contact listed in the form you submitted.

A PICS label encoded with the RSACI ratings will look something like this:

```
<META http-equiv="PICS-Label" content='(PICS-1.1 "http://
www.rsac.org/ratingsv01.html" l gen true comment "RSACi North
America Server" by "kgs@bluehighways.com" for "http://
www.bluehighways.com/tifap/" on "1997.08.30T12:22–0800"
r (n 0 s 0 v 0 l 1))'>
```

This may look like distracting gobbledygook, but focus on the last line, where you see:

r (n 0 s 0 v 0 l 1)

This is the RSACI content rating for this Website. The ratings are nudity 0, sex 0, violence 0, and language 1. (Other information in this metadata includes the PICS version, the rating system, who created the label, what the referent URL is, and the date and time of creation of this label.)

Without going into a long discussion about the meaning of each category, you can compare the label above with the Safe Surf label I generated from the Safe Surf Website:

<META http-equiv="PICS-Label" content='(PICS-1.1 "http://www.classify.org/safesurf/" l by "kgs@bluehighways.com" r (SS~~000 1 SS~~001 3 SS~~002 3 SS~~003 3))'>

With SafeSurf, I ended up identifying the TIFAP Website as safe for all ages, but with technical references to strong language, as well as heterosexual and homosexual behavior.

WHERE DO THESE LABELS GO?

Web authors can embed PICS labels into the unseen code at the top of their HTML documents, and third-party label bureaus (as they are called) can create databases of PICS labels. There can be an infinite number of PICS labels describing each resource. The rating systems, and the ratings, will be specific to the company or organization creating the label.

If you can have multiple labels for each document, in an Internet search, which of these labels determines what you can access? The answer is that it depends on which rating system the end-user (or the library) elects to use.

SO HOW DOES IT ACTUALLY WORK?

To limit Internet access to Websites that have been self-rated by the authors, and that include PICS labels in their own HTML source code, you need software enabled for PICS, and it needs to support the rating system you plan to use. Cyber Patrol, as mentioned earlier, supports RSACI and SafeSurf. Microsoft Explorer is technically open to any rating system, although it comes preconfigured for RSACI.

In Microsoft Explorer 3.02, if you go into Explorer's configuration panel (through View/Options), you can select a section called Security and then another section called Content Advisor. Within this section, you can select your rating service (which for this example will be RSACI), set up administrative passwords, decide whether to let through unrated Web pages, and set the RSACI levels you want to have access to.

If you are planning to experiment with PICS, configure your browser or filter software so you cannot go to unrated Websites. This is instructive. You will quickly notice that very few Websites have been self-rated. "Very few," on the Internet, may be in the tens of thousands, but that's still small beans compared to the huge amount of information on the Internet. Such staples of library service as the Census home page (http://www.census.gov) and The Internet Movie Database (http://www.imdb.com) did not have PICS labels in their source code as of this writing.

I'll give you a hand in locating a Website, assuming you want something other than the RSACI Website to play with (which is rated by its own system as 0,0,0,0, despite the presence of many terms it rates above these levels). The TIFAP webpage has two sets of metadata labels: one for RSACI and one for SafeSurf. As a reminder, the TIFAP Web page is at http://www.bluehighways.com/tifap/.

If you configure Explorer or Cyber Patrol so the user cannot view any page above RSACI level 0, then try to launch the URL for the TIFAP Web page, the page will not display. It is blocked because of the language rating 1 in its PICS label. If you set the RSACI levels higher, for example, to level 2 or 3, the page will now display.

If a label bureau existed, and you selected its services, its rating would be the one that determined whether or not you saw the TIFAP page.

PICS AND LIBRARIES

PICS was developed, and is discussed, around the issue of Internet content and children. Quite often PICS is recommended as a flexible way for parents and schools to control Internet content. And perhaps for these settings, where information retrieval takes a back seat to social control, PICS represents a real break-through, as long as the parent or teacher has high confidence in the fidelity of the labeling system.

For public-access environments such as libraries, PICS, in theory, offers some slight improvements over prevalent filtering software technologies.

The categories created by RSACI and SafeSurf are internally consistent, in the same way that LCSH and Sears headings, inside their own schemes, are internally consistent. This is an improvement over the wild variation among filter categories. For those of you who recall the days before AACR, the availability of several agreed-on standards will be immediately appreciated.

Additionally, while most Internet filters allow categories to be selectively enabled, PICS also allows a much more fine-tuned "sliding scale," at least with the RSACI rating system.

HOWEVER . . .

There is nothing compelling a label bureau to disclose its categories or make available its database of labels; in fact, as we have seen with filter vendors, since this is a value-added service, companies have every motivation for keeping these labels private. If PICS becomes an essential capability, I believe filter vendors will create their own rating systems and design their PICS capability around it. As I have said elsewhere in this book, it is hard to fault a business for protecting proprietary information; the point here is that PICS does not resolve the problem of hidden decisions about Internet content.

The intense pressure now placed on some libraries to use a particular solution for managing Internet content could easily transfer to community pressure to use a particular label bureau or even particular PICS settings. Current rating systems already demonstrate the influence of particular belief systems, such as the entire nudity category (which in some countries would appear strangely prudish) and SafeSurf's distinction between heterosexual and homosexual behavior.

And, of course, because they are inanimate objects incapable of critical thinking, PICS labels are unable to divine context, and rely on the rater's subjective judgment at the time the label was created. Our TIFAP tester found that Netshepherd's search engine blocked pharmaceutical information on oral contraceptives and a scientific paper on the effect of estrogenic disruptors on the genitalia of aquatic animals. If this is how rating systems perform when they try to be objective, what will they look like in the hands of those who do believe in enforcing their very specific beliefs in as many situations as possible? The rejoinder, that you can always select another label bureau, will only work if these label bureaus exist in the first place, and if at least one of them meets your requirement. (Government-imposed label bureaus, while a frightening concept, are hopefully not something we will ever see in a democratic country.)

As this book was being finished, news and media organizations had just signed a statement "strongly rejecting attempts to rate news sites on the Internet" (Yahoo News, http://www.yahoo.com/headlines/, "Hell No, We Won't Rate," August 30, 1997).

Self-rating, often touted as a compromise which allows the author to determine the rating of the document, has several limitations. First, as illustrated earlier, Web authors, even on major government and commercial sites, are not labeling themselves. Most Web authors ignore this extra step. Second, and perhaps related to the first, label bureaus can always override an author's label.

With current rating systems, PICS could only work if all Internet content is labeled. If it isn't labeled, the content you try to filter out will slip through if you have the software enabled to let through unrated sites, otherwise far too much content will be blocked. The prospect of actually labeling the entire Internet, and keeping such a label bureau current, is intriguing but not, without huge infusions of cash, feasible. As James LaRue wrote recently, "if libraries were to restrict World Wide Web offerings to rated sites, over 93% of Internet content would be eliminated." The only possible solution for this would be a rating system that focused on blocking pornography and nothing else, effectively letting the rest of the Internet "slip through" as unblocked sites.

If the entire Internet will not be fully rated at any one time, software for PICS must include meaningful user feedback. As a bottom line, end-users have the right to know what is blocked versus what has not been rated. Configured to block unrated sites, Netshepherd and Explorer display the same message whether a site is unrated or whether it is intentionally blocked. Not only does using the same message for all denials label unrated sites as "bad," but it fosters suspicion and concern. Netshepherd would give you the impression that it has an "agenda" against safe-sex information for teens; with unrated sites unblocked, it is clear that these sites have simply not been identified in the Netshepherd database. (Failure to include such well-known sites such as http://www.safersex.org, however, is worth pondering: which sites are rated first, and are some sites not selected at all?).

Finally, PICS does not address the resource-allocation and content management issues peculiar to libraries. While it is possible to imagine an encoding scheme that worked with other tools to help libraries implement decisions about time-outs, protocol denial, downloading, and other facts of life in the public-access environment, that is not the current focus of PICS, and we will continue to need separate tools for these purposes.

WHITHER PICS?

I don't know where PICS is going, and I'm not sure what it means for libraries; I don't think it's much of an improvement on the current situation. If you pointed a gun at my head and told me to make a useful compromise decision based on some form of control, I'd say I'd form a cooperative which would chip in on the gruntwork necessary to create a label bureau. I'd create a label targeted specifically at sexually-explicit material, and I'd have a stable of librarians working to identify as much Internet content as possible. The label bureau would be freely viewable to all cooperative members. The emphasis would be on ensuring libraries could access a wide spectrum of information while excluding the sexually explicit content that librarians find either inappropriate or unwise to offer.

In an ideal world, I would rather be working on interesting projects to develop new ways to find Internet content. But with a gun at your head, you do the best you can.

6

Advice from the Trenches: Librarians Share Their Experiences with Filters

IS THERE A RIGHT CHOICE?

Libraries are like snowflakes; no two are alike. There never will be a "one size fits all" solution. Nevertheless, we learn by sharing our stories, because we share similar goals and values.

In this chapter you will:

- Hear voices in the field talk about their experiences with filtering or not filtering; and
- Gain practical advice, from both librarians who filter and those who do not.

The common thread in all of these stories is that the librarians involved were proactive. They decided, ahead of time, whether to filter or not to filter, and then designed their actions around this decision. The actions ranged from placing privacy screens on computers, to developing a children's program for Internet use, to limiting access on some computers, to system-wide use of filters. In some cases, libraries chose to take very minimal action.

This is not to say that having a plan of attack, whether or not it includes filters, guarantees that a citizen's group will not show up one day with the media to make your life miserable over one book, one video, or one web page. However, strategic approaches to Internet content raise the odds (though do not guarantee) that you will be able to continue to manage your library without extensive interference from "out there." The better you have girded your loins, the better you can live with yourself, regardless of the outcome.

Whether or not you use a filter:

1 Get a clue. If you have yet to really learn about the Internet, do it now.

2 Be aware that there is material on the content which is sexually explicit, pornographic, obscene and/or illegal, and it is not hard to find

3 Make a decision about your plan of attack

4 Write a policy based on this decision

5 Communicate this policy ahead of time to your staff, your public and your funding/ managerial authorities

6 Have a clear, explicit plan for coping with challenges of all media

7 Communicate your actions—and your expectations—to staff

8 Review your decision frequently

9 Stay open to and respectful of all positions on this issue

CYBER KIDS: THE CANTON PUBLIC LIBRARY EXAMPLE

Special thanks to American Libraries for allowing me to quote extensively from my September, 1997 column on this topic.

Cyber Kids, an Internet program for children at the Canton Public Library, Michigan debuted in July, 1996. It is an example of how using policy, planning, user education, and public relations to provide guidelines for patron use of the Internet, can make debuting the Internet a tremendously successful experience for all involved.

Masterminded by Judy Teachworth, Youth Services Department Head, with the close assistance of library director Jean Tabor and Youth Services Librarian Wendy Woltjer, Cyber Kids has four crucial components:

1. An awareness and approval program,
2. A training and registration program for children,
3. A clear public-relations approach,
4. Carefully-constructed policies and procedures outlining what children can and can't do.

Parental Consent, and Buy-In from Kids

A Cyber Kids parent told the *Detroit News* last year, "I would highly recommend [the Cyber Kids program] to any parent." Part of the high comfort-level with Cyber Kids is due to the very explicit "Cyber Kids Consent Form" that is signed by both the parent and the child and retained at the library. This form has the parent acknowledge that the library "cannot act in loco parentis" and cautions the parent that the Internet "includes graphics and some controversial materials." The child must agree to follow the policies of the Cyber Kids Room and to "treat others with respect." If both parties sign the form, the library gives the child a Cyber Kids sticker. (Note that this is a low-cost, low-tech alternative to barcode support for access levels, discussed in Chapter 3, "Filter Features.")

User Education

The next step to becoming a Cyber Kid is an "Orientation Session"—a half-hour parent-child introduction to the Internet, conducted by library staff. Not surprisingly (at least to those of us who offer Internet training for our clientele), the parents often benefit from Internet training as well; a typical comment afterwards is "Wow! I didn't know all that stuff was out there."

These training sessions also offer parents and children Internet safety guidelines, and the librarian instructors reinforce the "Cyber Rules" for using the Internet workstations. These rules include placing the Cyber Kids sticker in a pocket on the computer, always wearing headphones, and the big rule that, as the Cyber Kids brochure bluntly states it, "if you break your Cyber Kid agreement, you will lose your privileges."

Public Relations and the Cyber Kids Brochure

Little details count, particularly in public relations. One such detail is the media program. Judy Teachworth pointed toward the city-wide mailings and local press coverage. The Cyber Kids brochure is also key. This publication markets the program and reminds readers of the guidelines for use. Library brochures grow legs and walk far, in my experience.

Key details from Cyber Kids:

- A consent form adults and children sign together
- Parent-child classes
- Careful use of public relations
- An intentional search area and procedures for using it

Strategic Equipment

Other details to note are in the physical arrangement of the Cyber Kids Room. This includes a "neon sign which proclaims CYBER KIDS in large letters," as director Jean Tabor told me. Other physical details include placing the youth reference desk near the Cyber Kids Room, and adding two bulletin boards—one for announcements, and one for kids to post their favorite sites and games.

Of course, just equipping the room right in the first place counts, too. The Cyber Kids Room has seven computers—which probably doesn't seem like a lot on a busy afternoon, but is more computing ability than many comparably-sized libraries have in their entire building. (Cyber Kids was funded from the Library's general budget and with a one-time gift from the Friends of the Library.) Generous access is part of the strategy; one of the reasons Cyber Kids exists is to "provide access for children who do not have access to the Internet [at home]," and another is "to educate future users."

Even if you do choose to filter, a program such as Cyber Kids can go a long way toward building information-responsible library users.

David Burt's Policy Archive

David Burt, an Internet services librarian at Lake Oswego Public Library, Oregon, has an excellent selection of library policies on his library's website. See:

http://www.ci.oswego.or.us/library/poli.htm

ENGLEWOOD PUBLIC LIBRARY: SELECTIVE USE OF FILTERS

Filters on the Children's Room Computers

Director Hank Long of Englewood Public Library (one building and one bookmobile in a town of 30,000) told me that his library uses Cyber Patrol on the two workstations in the children's area and does not use filtering software on the six workstations in the adult area. "At the same time," Hank told me, "our staff will NOT tell kids they cannot use the adult terminals," and librarians warn parents "who choose to use the two filtered terminals" that filters are not "foolproof."

Englewood Public Library uses a variety of techniques to alert users that computers are filtered and educate users in Internet issues. Signs are posted over the children's Internet computers informing users that these machines are filtered and encouraging parents to work with children in selecting acceptable sites. Near these computers, parents and children will find "Dear Parents" bookmarks, which discuss parental responsibility in helping children select appropriate materials in every medium. Here you will also find copies of "Child Safety on the Information Superhighway," a pamphlet produced by the National Center for Missing and Exploited Children. "Most importantly," added Hank, "we talk face-to-face with those parents who have concerns about the Internet."

Library Board Buy-In; Two Kinds of Access

The Library Board made the decision to use filtering software in the children's room (and not in the adult area), and Hank Long agrees with them. The Board felt that this was an "acceptable" solution "for those people who want some form of control when their kids visit the library, while providing full, open access to parents, and kids with approving parents, who don't want to have their access filtered."

Strategic Planning and Political Savvy

"By taking this action," added Hank, "I feel we may also keep at arm's length those 'family friendly' folk who try to use 'Internet pornography' as an excuse to get their fascist feet in the public library door." Hank said this was a "compromise," but added, "and we make compromises every day of the week. Is it a perfect answer? No. Is it politically savvy? Yes."

MONROE COUNTY PUBLIC LIBRARY: POLICY, PROCEDURE, AND STAFF TRAINING

The Difference Between Policy and Practice

This story will ring a bell with anyone who has ever coped with the sometimes-wide gulf between policy and practice.

Note in the Englewood example:

- Selective use of filters
- Also offering unfiltered access
- Library Board buy-in
- A preemptive strike against special-interest groups who may use the "net porn" scare to further other agendas

Monroe County Public Library has a strong policy, carefully worded, that explains patron behavior and the library's decision not to use blocking software. The policy was distributed through several channels:

- The public computing center
- Staff policy manuals
- The library website

However, while librarians at Monroe County Public Library generally agreed that filtering was not appropriate in their library, staff were still uncertain about whether "to approach patrons viewing what might be considered inappropriate sites," said Lisa Champelli of MCPL, a children's librarian and, with Dr. Howard Rosenbaum, co-author of the *Neal-Schuman Webmaster* (Neal-Schuman, 1997). Staff felt that "unless the person's behavior was problematic...they did not want to be put in the position of whether to negotiate with patrons." Lisa added, "a policy is only as effective as the people involved in interpreting or enforcing it." Lisa and another librarian, Chris Jackson, were instrumental in developing and implementing MCPL's policy.

Crossing the Divide: The Implementation Plan

MCPL's efforts to educate staff about the policy, intellectual freedom issues, and how to implement the policy in real life included:

- A discussion list created for staff to share questions and concerns about Internet use at MCPL

- A special staff meeting for explaining the policy and proposed procedures for implementing it
- A communications training session, including role-playing activities, to help staff members who may be called on to explain the policy to patrons
- A list of procedures for supporting the policy, such as signs advising patrons to log out of sessions and return their browsers to "home" when they were through

All told, Lisa and Chris worked hard to create an environment that dealt with the realities of patron and librarian behavior while preserving MCPL's commitment to not use blocking software.

ASKING PATRONS TO COOL IT: BOULDER CITY LIBRARY DISTRICT

One part of the MCPL training included what to do when librarians observed patrons violating the policy. In some libraries, staff are not comfortable approaching patrons to explain that they are violating library policy—and won't become comfortable, regardless of training sessions, policies and the like. Whether your staff can and will approach patrons violating library policies is something you either know or will find out through experimentation. It's useless to take a very hard line on this if the particular work environment won't support it. As Marvin Scilken, editor of *The Unabashed Librarian*, once told me, "anything the staff doesn't like will be lost or broken."

On the other hand, in some settings, telling patrons to refrain from viewing inappropriate material is what librarians are doing, and it works for them. Duncan McCoy, Director of the Boulder City Library District, says that his library has had "several incidents of youngsters and one of an adult accessing porn websites. In each case, we asked the patron to back out of the website and focus on something else. They didn't fuss about it." This wasn't an ad-hoc decision, but a deliberate choice to approach the problem this way.

Regarding asking patrons to refrain from looking at sexually-explicit images, Duncan explained his library's philosophy: that other patrons should not have to be exposed to "graphic skin pictures" and that except for real research in this area, pornography is "a nonissue and not worth fighting our community about."

In his library, Duncan concluded, "porn is not a problem because we've evolved a procedure for dealing with it that seems to be effective in our community. Doesn't happen all that often, and when it does, it's sort of on the level of our having to ask patrons to quiet down or check their Slurpie at the desk."

AUSTIN PUBLIC LIBRARY: SWIFT RESPONSE TO PRECIPITATING INCIDENTS

Austin Public Library had two precipitating incidents which were enough for them to decide to filter Internet computers. One incident involved someone printing obscene graphics of adults having sex with kids. Another incident involved an adult showing children how to access pornography.

Note: Sometimes libraries use filters when what they really want is software that can automatically :

- Time-out a session

- Empty the history list of a browser

- Return the browser's webpage to a main page when the session is through

---

As Frank Bridge, system programming manager for Austin Public Library, told me, "you have to use your best judgment using the best information at the time." Their judgment was, use filters; in Texas, both incidents violated statutes, and politically as well as geographically, it's a long drive from Boulder to Austin. Due to a complicated political relationship with a local community network which provides the computers housed in the libraries, server-based software was not feasible. So they installed 50 copies of Cyber Patrol. Maintaining this client software has been labor-intensive, but, they felt, worth the effort.

Initially Austin Public Library started at the highest settings for Cyber Patrol, then "tweaked" the software back after patron complaints revealed the software was blocking a lot of good information. As Frank said, there's still an error rate in both directions (good resources blocked and "bad stuff" let through), but for now, they're in equilibrium.

Frank told me that if you don't need to use filters—don't use them. "It's just one more thing you gotta mess with." In their case, though, Cyber Patrol has met their needs, and they have configured it in a way that results in very few patron complaints. With very little information to go on, they made a decision they could live with.

PRIVACY SCREENS

MCPL is one of several libraries that talked to me about privacy screens. These are used to provide privacy for computer users from casual passers-by. This works both ways: first, the person using the Internet can have the same privacy to seek, for example, confidential medical information; second, passers-by cannot easily see what the person is viewing.

These sound ideal, but librarians with experience with privacy screens report some problems. The screens tend to smudge, they are hard to secure to the computer (one librarian informed me their screen was stolen the day it was installed), they are not cheap, and some people (including me) find they really obstruct what is viewable on a computer screen. Additionally, Eloise May of Arapahoe Library District in Littleton, Colorado, echoed several people who wrote me to say that these screens interfere with group computing activities so common in libraries—librarian-patron, groups of students, parent-child, and so forth. These screens also aren't designed for frequent removal and replacement; maybe if they swung on a sturdy clip, like my beloved Rubbermaid computer-monitor copyholder, they would be a little more worthy of intensive public use.

COMPUTER ARRANGEMENT

Librarians often discuss strategically arranging computers to allow patrons more privacy and to prevent passers-by from being forced to see what users are viewing. Sometimes this works, and sometimes it doesn't. There are any number of libraries with one or two computers; classrooms and labs may have computers locked into particular arrangements. Furthermore, in some rooms, such as children's rooms in large urban libraries, the expectation is that adults *are* closely observing what is happening at the computers. In one library I worked in, we had a locked bathroom and mirrors in each eave

---

One Source for Privacy Screens

3M Privacy Plus Anti-Glare Filter, available for under $100 from office and library supply stores and catalogs.

Search the 3M website for the latest models:
http://www.mmm.com/

Thanks to Eloise May of Arapahoe Library District, Colorado, for this information!

---

of the room, designed to deter pedophiles (something I have no apologies for).

Finally, as Chris Jackson of MCPL wrote me, "most of [the computers in the library are] used to access a variety of resources . . . and if users are having trouble with these resources, we'd like to be able to make eye contact." While computer arrangement should be considered, and can be a help, it will rarely be a sole solution.

General Advice for Anyone Implementing Public Access to the Internet

Karen Hyman, of the South Jersey Regional Library Cooperative, provided this perspective after a year of using a filter in her regional library network. Her advice works equally well whether you are planning to use a filter or not!

1. **Get the facts and question authority.** Don't take legal opinions from a techie. Don't get technical information from a lawyer. Have a healthy sense of skepticism about anything you read or hear, especially "factual" information offered to bolster an ideological point of view. Realize that when it comes to what the courts will say or what the technology will do in the future, only the clairvoyant know for sure.
2. **Stop looking for the perfect choice.** All choices are flawed. Try a commonsense approach that has some potential for fulfilling your mission and working with your staff and users.
3. **Focus on customer service.** Internet access is a customer service issue. Few terminals, a slow connection, little or no staff assistance and a plethora of tedious, hoop-jumping rules restrict access more significantly than filtering porn—they affect everybody all of the time.

Tweaking Software Is a Must

In TIFAP, two of the three predictors of performance were whether keyword blocking was disabled, and whether the software was "tweaked" to target only sexually-explicit material.

How to tweak Cyber Patrol (based on Version 3.0):

Courtesy of Myron Estelle, Cumberland County Libraries

Objective: to configure Cyber Patrol with these settings: Disable PICS restrictions. Disable all categories except Full Nudity. Disable keyword blocking.

Step 1: On opening screen select Site Control (at upper left), select PICS RSACi Rating Setup. At lower left, put x in box next to Disable RSACi. Click on Save. Close.

Step 2: Go back to Site Control. Select PICS SafeSurf Setup. At lower left, put x in box next to Disable SafeSurf. Click on Save. Close.

Step 3: Under CyberPatrol Logo, Click on categories. Click on each box to remove x's. Leave x next to Full Nudity. Click on Save my selections. Close.

Step 4: At headquarters screen, Click on ChatGard at upper right. At lower right, put x in box next to Disable ChatGard. Click on Save Changes and close.

Step 5: At headquarters screen, Click on WWW, FTP & other. At lower left, click on box in front of Apply IRC Wild Card filters to URL names to REMOVE x.
    Click on Save Changes and close.

Step 6: Test to see if you've been successful, try a netsearch on "atrial fibrillation". If you get BLOCKED BY CYBERPATROL, you're still applying IRC Wildcard Filters. Check to be sure you saved your changes or reboot. Try a netsearch on Matsushita. If what you typed turns out like Matsuxxxxa, Chat Guard is still on. Check to be sure you have saved your changes and reboot.

4. **Start a dialogue.** – Talk with staff, governing agencies, library users, vendors, and colleagues in the profession. Ask questions and listen to the answers. If we want a product that is a better fit for the library market, we're going to have to tell vendors what we want.

5. **Remember that we are not the center of the universe.** The big power brokers could change the picture tomorrow. Our strength is in our knowledge, creativity, ethics and ability to forge common ground—among ourselves and with others.

   And especially for those who are filtering in a limited, careful, and responsible way:

6. **Stop apologizing.**

What a Filter Cannot Do

- A filter cannot substitute for library policy

- A filter cannot guarantee that anyone will never see "bad stuff" on the Internet (however you define it)

- A filter cannot substitute for staff training

- A filter cannot substitute for communicating with your user population

- A filter cannot show people what is good about the Internet

PART II:
EVALUATING AVAILABLE FILTERS

7

Learning from The Internet Filter Assessment Project

Project Website:
http://www.bluehighways.com/tifap/

A list of all the active volunteers and their roles in this project is in the acknowledgement at the beginning of this book. The project questions are in Appendix A.

The Internet Filter Assessment Project (TIFAP) ran from April to September, 1997. It was a volunteer project involving close to 40 librarians. I was the project manager. We ran this product by email and over the Web. In this strictly print-oriented medium, I did not even know how to pronounce the project name until June, when a friend and TIFAP volunteer, George Porter, dined with me and informed me that it was pronounced "TIFF-app."

TIFAP arose from questions and concerns librarians had about the use of filters in libraries. Some of the volunteers were "pro," some were "anti," some were uncertain, but all were of the mindset that you don't know a tool until you use it. My own concern was that the site lists are nearly always private. Interestingly, this isn't an issue this project could ever directly address.

TIFAP had four goals for the library community at large and this author in particular:

1. To shape a features list, which eventually became the criteria you see in this book
2. To demonstrate how filters perform better at minimal settings
3. To identify levels of comfort and discomfort with a variety of Internet content
4. To demonstrate the value of testing filters

TIFAP is generally misunderstood as strictly a product assessment, but that is not its real value. TIFAP was not primarily useful for drawing very specific conclusions about individual products (though the product-specific information that did arise from TIFAP has been echoed in many other corners). Vendors, in particular, have misunderstood this, and have called and written to ask me "what the results will say about their product." On several occasions vendors have implied that anything I say about their product in this book or elsewhere will be *a priori* tainted because TIFAP was, as I am honest enough to state clearly, unscientific. (However, the filter reviews that occasionally crop up in computer magazines are equally unscientific but, unlike TIFAP, useless for library settings).

TIFAP and the (Un)Scientific Method

TIFAP was not a scientific study; it lacked controls, the actual conditions could not be verified, and, due to limited volunteers and resources, we could not consistently test all products the same way. The survey instruments are as amateurish as you would expect from people who do not design surveys.

However, in terms of conclusions about specific products, TIFAP is no less valid than a vendor's claims, a personal assessment, or a software magazine's review. Our most significant assessment is that you should test the filter under your local public access conditions—nothing else will substitute. The very heterogeneity of the librarians evaluating filters ensured that TIFAP is inherently more valid, for library purposes, than any other product assessment now available.

Most of the librarians worked closely with me, each other, and the vendors to ensure that the product was properly configured. When misconfigurations were found, or new features came available, we reconfigured and retested.

How TIFAP Worked

There were several components to TIFAP. First, we developed test questions we felt would be good for seeing how filters performed in real life. A filter vendor recently commented that the questions listed in the back of this book seemed very realistic; that's because many of them are real reference questions from the front lines of librarianship. The URLs we tested became stale very quickly (though they are still available on the TIFAP Website). The filter vendors eventually discovered most of the naughty URLs, and some of the good ones moved. The questions, however, retain their usefulness as excellent tools for evaluating filter performance, both in the area of keyword blocking and in the area of what filters rate as "bad," and you are encouraged to make whatever use of them you can.

Next, we developed a survey to test filters, and assigned librarians to particular filters. We put a form on the webpage that sent files to me. TIFAP "unfiltered" volunteers first assessed questions in an unfiltered environment, both to ensure they were answerable and to see what happens when you look up information (in terms of retrieving objectionable information, with the understanding that this term is infinitely subjective).

After discussion, I decreed that we should "search like librarians," because that's what we are, and it's not something we can pretend not to be. That's a known limitation in TIFAP, for two reasons. First, librarians can search more precisely. Librarians often claim they never see pornography on the Internet, and I believe them; they are a) focused on their work, and b) very good searchers capable of high precision with their first search query. Much of the queries, which were captured in the survey results, featured nested Boolean searches, with extensive "and"-ing (e.g., (+beaver +dam) not sex*). Second, librarians can search more strategically and creatively than the typical end user. The librarian who knew to search for "erectile dysfunction" ran a very clever end run around the blocked term "penis" in the question about penile implants. You can learn a lot by studying analog artificial intelligence exception-handling units (that is, librarians); search strategies used by TIFAP testers are on the project Website.

Then the day came when I said "go" and we began what we called Phase 2 testing: assessing these filters, whenever possible, at "full throttle" (all settings enabled, including keyword blocking) to see how they performed. We tested over 100 questions we had developed. Seven filters were tested at "full" settings, with all blocking enabled, including keyword blocking: Bess, Cyber Patrol, Cyber Snoop, Cybersitter, Net Nanny, NetShepherd, and Surfwatch. Two filters were also tested with "Lite" settings (blocking only full and partial nudity in Cyber Patrol, and only pornography and chat groups in Websense). A product, The Library Channel, which bills itself as a selection tool, was also evaluated in this phase. Testers submitted answers via an email form. Over 400 forms were submitted in this phase.

Then I culled almost 200 URLs gathered from this stage—those that had been blocked, when this was known, and those that had been let through. The TIFAP team created another survey, designed to see how filters perform on URLs when filters are set to minimal settings with keyword blocking disabled—and how librarians reacted to these URLs. Over 700 survey forms were submitted for the URL tests (known as "Phase 3").

Meanwhile, after attempting to consolidate information manually, I realized that the best way to manage data for TIFAP was through a survey program, so I bought a program (SurveySaid) and began keying in forms. This was slow going for the 700 Phase 3 forms, but much quicker for the earlier, Phase 2 forms.

Finally, librarians were encouraged to assess the filters on their own and provide summaries of their impressions to me. We developed a preliminary criteria list, which was key source material for this book.

TIFAP and I can only take part of the credit for this criteria. A major nod must go to Jerry Kuntz of the Ramapo Catskill Library System. Earlier in 1997, Jerry conducted his own project to identify criteria for filter assessment, which this project borrowed heavily from, and Jerry also conducted a survey of filter vendors which was an important resource for the product feature section. Jerry's LibraryLand has an excellent section on Internet filters, including links to his vendor surveys, at http://www.rcls.org/libland/cen/cens.htm.

A special thank-you to the vendors is due. Sometimes the filters we looked at were already installed in the libraries where they were being tested; other times, vendors very kindly donated copies of their product or, as in the case of Bess and I-Gear, provided access to remote proxy servers. Technical support staff patiently answered questions, provided documentation, and walked librarians through the travails of new software installation, maintenance, use, and removal. The vendor support for this project was close to remarkable.

After these results were tabulated, I culled as many URLs as I could decipher from the results—over 200—and created lists of

URLs (representing a broad spectrum, from bland government sites to hardcore porn), and the testers went at it again. This time the focus was on performance with keyword blocking disabled. With the filter categories "full on," but keyword blocking disabled, we looked at Bess, Cyber Patrol, I-Gear, and Net Nanny. Websense and Smart Filter were also tested, but at "Lite" settings (blocking pornography only). Library Channel was again evaluated.

WHAT ARE THE LESSONS LEARNED?

Configure Filters

First, for these filters to be useful in library settings, we found that keyword blocking and most of the categories need to be disabled—so as to approximate a filter that blocked sexually-explicit material, and only sexually-explicit material. Tweaking filters wasn't a new idea; librarians using filters had already discovered this through trial and error. However, it was still good to know that tweaking is better than not tweaking, because not all filters let you disable keyword blocking, and not all filters have categories that can be selectively enabled. In other words, tweakability is important.

How do filters perform at full throttle? Badly, if information is your goal. In the first test phase, 78% of the time, librarians found what they were looking for. However, when they couldn't, it was often true that the filter was blocking information, as well. Over 35% of the time, the filters blocked some information they needed to answer a question. Keyword blocking obscured everything from nursery rhymes ("pussycat, pussycat"—blocked repeatedly, even, in one case, when the tester used the search terms "nursery rhymes") to government physics archives (the URL began with XXX) to the word "button" (obscured by Cybersitter in an email message).

Keyword settings aside, the filters also blocked sites with information similar to what would be found in libraries—Websites for hate groups, press releases on sex offenders, an interview with Leslea Newman, an organization for gay teens, a list of jockeys, safe sex information, pros and cons on the legalization of drugs, and so forth. In other words, the filters worked as advertised: they blocked information related to a wide variety of issues. Think about it: at some point you probably expended labor to select material in one of these categories—and now you can pay someone to deselect it!

The ability to configure the filter is therefore very significant. When the answer was "yes" to the first test's question, "Did you find what you were looking for," the "Lite" settings outperformed other filters by over 20%, in one case putting the filter at over 97% on this question. This question is related to the tester's searching skills, and these were very good.

Site Lists Are Important

I have said, in the past, that libraries interested in blocking pornography should develop their own lists. I stand extremely corrected. To gather a working list of all known pornographic sites is not the occasional work of one busy information professional, but requires intensive attention from a dedicated team. Net Nanny, which advertises the value of being able to build one's own site lists, includes perfunctory and outdated lists that performed very poorly at blocking pornography when keyword blocking was disabled. The sometimes outlandish claims vendors make for their keyword blocking (or, in the snake-oil lingo of several packages, "intuitive content recognition") exist because paying a programmer to develop a keyword-blocking capability is still cheaper than paying full-time staff salary and benefits.

Whether you believe in blocking pornography is another story. If you want to do it well, at present, you will have to pay a company that pays people to collect bad sites all day. The site list will be hidden, and it will have mistakes. It's up to you to decide whether you can live with this and if so, to what extent.

It's the Pornography, Stupid (And the Kids)

Over 10% of the time, librarians said they wanted complete or conditional blocks in answer to the following question: "Imagine that you saw the webpage for this URL or its related URLs on a computer in your library. How would you want the filter to perform?" The breakdown was 6% unconditional block, and 4% conditional block, where age was the condition. Within the age breakdown, this was always either for 18 and above (60%) or 7 and below (40%), with not one selection for 12 and below.

For all the discussion about what folks don't want people accessing at public computers in libraries, as far as adult users go, it boils down to this: pornography. If TIFAP testers emphatically wanted a site blocked for all viewers, adult and child alike, 84% of the time, that was due to sexually explicit content. If they wanted it blocked conditionally—either for the under-18 or under-7 crowd—those reasons were more scattered, and were distributed across foul language, drug promotion, etc, but sexually-explicit information still took the lead at 30%. Based on the comments testers put in their forms, furthermore, the level of enthusiasm for blocking was reserved for sexually explicit material. "I could let this one slide" was written more than once in a comments field about a non-sexual site the tester felt should be conditionally blocked.

Many testers did not have a problem with blocking sexually-explicit information while justifying access to all other kinds of information by checking a box next to, "Librarians should not block free speech." Even the most ardent "First Amendment" tester, who resolutely never wanted to block anything, had a very interesting pattern. When the material was not sexually explicit, this tester selected four reasons why the information should not be blocked (free speech, shouldn't block the Internet, tester's own standards, community standards); when the information *was* sexually explicit, the tester selected only one reason—free speech.

Sex Questions: The Presumption of Prurience

Reference questions about sex were harder to answer, probably because more related sites are blocked. Only 64% of the sex questions (category 1) were answered successfully, while answers in the other categories were in the 80th and 90th percentiles.

Not only that, but when information was completely blocked, more than half the time the tester assumed that the information was sexually-explicit. In Phase 2, we did not instruct testers to view their sites unfiltered (as we did in Phase 3), so they were often assuming that information was sexually-explicit simply because it was blocked. This is a natural assumption, based on how these filters perform, but it points up another problem with using a tool that is designed to block "bad stuff." We need to think carefully about sending a message that anything inaccessible is inherently bad. Again, we need better monitoring capabilities, and we need to focus on the twin issues of outsourcing selection decisions to third parties, and privatizing the information that is blocked.

Freedom of Expression: User Feedback and Filters

Feedback mechanisms were not always up to snuff. If someone reaches a site that is blocked, they deserve a better answer than "Cyber Patrol Code 2," which is in turn better than software that disrupts page transmission, closes down the browser or obliterates words in Web pages. Some filters let you change the messages users see; some don't. Links to email—to suggest reconsideration, for example—aren't always provided, either.

Sometimes vendors provide user-feedback capability and librarians disable it, or set up their filters so they do silent redirects rather than notifying patrons of blocks; this was true in one tester's setting. If you are turning part of the Internet into closed stacks, at least let folks know what you're doing.

It's Porn . . . No, It's Adult Entertainment . . . No, It's Porn

As a librarian, I have pondered how one master database could meet every community need, and I have speculated that (particularly in areas that are less clear than very hard pornography) filter companies may be adding and deleting the same URLs. I discuss the problem of a master database in Chapter 3, "Filter Features."

You Aren't Guaranteed Anything

If you disable most of the blocking features in a filter, it will let through more of the stuff you are trying to block. There is also the problem of sites being misidentified and blocked as well. One filter, at full settings, blocked a government brochure on the dangers of cocaine and let through a site describing in full detail how to make cocaine. After watching filters for months, I don't think, most of the time, there are nefarious plans afoot; but if a site is unreachable, it doesn't matter if it's a slip or it's intentional—the bottom line is that the information is inaccessible, and it has just been labeled, by inference, inappropriate by local standards.

Even in the first test, over 8% of what the testers accessed they determined was "objectionable"; in the second test, testers wanted to block about 5% of what they saw. (I attribute the lower number to two reasons: this was an aging set of URLs, and one never-block tester who had not participated in the first test). Filters can't block what they don't know about, which is why some filters come with keyword blocking built in; it costs money to build those site lists, and keyword blocking means in theory you need fewer people because the software will block it on the fly. (Keyword blocking doesn't work, as we discovered, in any meaningful information setting.)

There are technical issues at play here, as well. Some filters can only block or enable entire domains, so anything on a site with content the filter is blocking becomes friendly fire. Again, the filter doesn't tell you why this is happening; from the end-user's perspective, there is just something "bad" there. Even the better products can be stumped by a Website where the host directory contains sexually-explicit material and subdirectories do not.

Librarian Search Behavior

In Phase 2, 94% of the time librarians used a search engine, and were least likely to find a resource if they didn't. This (which is also no surprise) has several implications. I have been one of the proponents of building nice guides and encouraging folks to use them, but people don't function that way; they—and we—want powerful search tools. Also, tools such as The Library Channel, designed around extensive "drill down" behavior—following categories of materials—may work well for librarians, who think that way, but are not likely to work well for the general public, who do not. I stand corrected, and any tool built on this presumption needs to be tested in a real user environment.

Software Performance Issues

The client-based software bedeviled testers by interfering with other software, rewriting key program files, refusing to uninstall, creating mysterious transient problems, or just by being very difficult to configure. It's fine to talk about "tweaking" filters, but even with extensive human help, some very computer-literate testers had trouble doing so.

Configuration and Authentication Issues

Most filters do not have configuration and authentication services truly robust enough for library systems. Some are coming close, but their pressure point is apparently the business industry, not librarians. There are probably many libraries out there using filters at this point; we don't know how many. There are certainly enough to get the features they wanted if they asked for them. Librarians have suggested that they would like a patron override option (warn-versus-block) for adult users; vendors have said they can implement this; it's a matter of being a savvy enough consumer (or not under intense pressure) to ask for what you want. With the client software, however, there are so few options that we are apparently stuck with one or at best two products, giving us less room to negotiate.

Final Thoughts

No report or study could capture the very special personal discoveries of the group as a whole: lessons about teamwork, about sharing, about being proactive, about the value of discovery.

This was a long journey for the TIFAP crowd. Everyone had an awakening of some sort or another. In some cases, filters performed better than people thought they would; in other cases, worse. Only one filter, Cybersitter, was completely unsatisfactory; some others could not be configured with keyword blocking disabled and categories set minimally; some seemed to consistently perform better than others.

The strongest predictor of filter performance, however, was a feature you should take into account: the person using the computer. The only way you know if a filter will work in your situation is to test it first. These are mechanical tools wrapped around subjective judgment, and you are paying someone to answer the question, "what's bad about this resource?"

Don't Ever Buy Software You Don't Need

If you don't need a filter, don't spend the money (which you will spend many times over in maintenance, as well). You do need to make an intentional decision not to use filters, because failure to be proactive with your decision, as I discuss in Chapter 6, "Advice from the Trenches," will catch up with you. But no matter what someone says, if filtering isn't the right direction for your library—don't go there. Would you bother with a software purchase you don't need, particularly when the bulk of the purchase price goes toward maintaining site blocks on the type of information you work hard to provide in other library settings? Would you put on a sweater, if you weren't cold?

If you do think you must use a filter in your situation—and I believe most TIFAP testers felt enormous empathy for the library that wanted to filter as well as the library that felt it should filter—look before you leap, and be willing to change your mind midair. If you are thinking about using a filter, but it does not meet your needs, tell the vendors what you want, and tell your funding authorities why you are waiting.

8

Product Reviews

In this section I present product reviews for major products now on the market. Some of the information comes from TIFAP evaluators; a lot of it comes also from me; information in italics was vendor-supplied.

These products vary widely in performance—sometimes within products, as well. Before discussing these products, I'd like to entertain ideas about what a better filter would look like.

TOWARD A BETTER FILTER

First of all, such a filter would block only targeted content. In libraries, that appears to be, for the most part, sexually-explicit information. Our education in online searching, and our experience with specialized databases, should be helpful in understanding that a product that focuses on one area will have more precision and granularity than a product that attempts to be all things to all people.

The KISS Principle and Filters

Some librarians may respond that they want to limit access to other information, as well. To this, we need to ask: why? If it's not illegal, and it isn't so sexually explicit that it exceeds those already-vague standards we're struggling with, why should librarians limit access to it? At this point, we are indulging in social engineering—

redesigning the Internet to promote our own views of the world.

I do understand that in our culture, depictions of uninhibited sexuality push so many buttons and set off so many alarms that most of us would rather not deal with it. I also suspect that most producers of sexually-explicit information are not going to fight for the right to display their wares in public libraries. However, the First-Amendment hard-liners have one very good point: once we block some information, we start sliding down a slippery slope. Most of us, I think, can agree in general what truly hardcore pornography entails. That's a slope, but it isn't too steep. The other areas, however tempting, are not worth turning that slope into a precipice where we tumble quickly toward censorship.

There are Websites that push my own buttons. When I shared my thoughts with a fairly conservative TIFAP volunteer, she reminded me that some of the sites that upset me the most only included opinions. Her comments reminded me of my commitment to providing access to information. It can be tough to buy, catalog and circulate—or even recommend—books we don't agree with, but when we do, we know we are ensuring all sides of an issue are available. It's important to apply the same standards of selection to Internet resources.

Librarians Aren't Cops

Sometimes it is suggested that a "good" feature for a filter would be that it blocked illegal content. For example, recently there was a proposal to outlaw using the Internet to distribute bomb-making information. Fine; I hope our enforcement agencies are doing their work to deal with this. We are not, nor should we be obliged to enforce laws at the local level any more than we expect librarians to arm themselves to cope with local crime. If it's truly illegal, the enforcement agencies should do their jobs. If they can't, we have a bigger problem than a few dozen files on the Internet. Imposing this task on a software program, or the people who use it, is unrealistic.

It's not the Internet we should be policing; it's these tools we know so little about. These tools should have good monitoring and reporting capabilities and feedback messages that provide as much information to users as possible about decisions others are making on their behalf.

Put It on the Table

Finally, a filter should not hide what it is doing. We cannot make filter companies accountable for their actions as long as this information is private. My concern about private site lists is a hobbyhorse I have ridden for most of this book. The only possible solution I have come up with is an anathema to many librarians: we could make our own list of sites to block—collectively funded, and collectively available. I have said to filter vendors that other features they offer—resource allocation, workstation control, and so forth—are valuable technologies, but that content is their weakness. I have also pointed out that we often buy empty databases strictly on the strength of their abilities to manage information (as in the case of OPACs). Finally, I think a list we create ourselves would be a bit shorter than a list created by vendors. This is my "capital punishment" theory: my feeling about capital punishment depends a lot on whether or not I would have to actually kill the person I condemn to death. I suspect most librarians would err on the side of access in evaluating Websites for exclusion. That may sound horrific—librarians as censors—but that's what we're doing when we outsource this task to companies, and in a sense, we're asking someone else to throw the switch.

WHAT THE FEATURE TABLES MEAN

All of these features are discussed in earlier chapters. The comments below are designed as "ticklers" to remind you of key points.

Feature 1: Vendor-supplied Site List
Feature 2: Number of Staff Maintaining List

These features are meaningless outside of the context of blocking performance, which is discussed in the product reviews.

Feature 3: View Site List
Feature 4: Edit Site List

Only two products allowed customers to view or edit the site lists (not to be confused with viewing or editing local lists maintained by the customer).

Feature 5: Site List Update Frequency

This refers to how often the company provides new information to the customer, not to how often the company updates its own information.

Feature 6: Automated List Download

This means downloading the site list can be scheduled to be done automatically, without further action from the customer.

Feature 7: Support Third-Party Lists

More significant questions would be "how" and "what lists," but if the vendor indicates this is a possibility, then you can discuss the particulars.

Feature 8: Local Access/Deny Lists

In addition to the existence of these essential features, find out if the filter allows you to create lists by category, and how many items a list can hold.

Feature 9: Keyword Filtering
Feature 10: Disable Keyword Filtering

As noted repeatedly in earlier discussions, keyword blocking is a feature you want to be able to turn off. The complete absence of keyword blocking in a product indicates that it is relying exclusively on blocking by sites, which is a desirable feature.

Feature 11: Block to File Level

Blocking to the file level means http://www.foobird.com/happy.html can be blocked while http://www.foobird.com/sad.html can be left unblocked.

Feature 12: Block by Protocol

This refers to the ability to block a specific Internet tool. This might be completely (as in, disabling chat) or selectively (disabling URLs). Note that "chat" is a conglomeration of protocols.

Definitions of Protocols

These acronyms are usually written lower case.

ftp: File Transfer Protocol: downloading and uploading files on the Internet; downloading is usually integrated into browsers

gopher: Simple, hierarchical information service, not used much any more

http: Hypertext Transfer Protocol; the Web

irc: Internet Relay Chat.

nntp: Network News Transport Protocol; the protocol for Usenet

smtp: Simple Mail Transport Protocol: email traffic

telnet: simple character-based remote logins

Feature 13: Block by Time of Day

This feature should not be confused with time-outs; it refers to time periods when the filter is active or blocks access entirely.

Feature 14: Host Resolves to IP
Feature 15: Support Time-outs

Most filters support blocking the IP addresses of hostnames; none at writing supported time-outs (ending after a predetermined period).

Feature 16: Configure by IP Address

At minimum, this meant that if two computers passed Internet traffic through the proxy server, one could be set to block and the other could be "clear channel" (jargon for unfiltered access). More fine-tuned configuration was supported by a couple of filters.

Feature 17: Configure by User ID
Feature 18: Support Patron Barcodes

Very few filters support Feature 17, and none support Feature 18, though vendors indicated interest in these features, pending market demand. Additionally, barcodes could be used in lieu of patron IDs, though without the barcode-reader capability.

Feature 19: Vendor-defined Categories
Feature 20: Block or Enable by Categories

The number of categories is indicated in the column. Having many categories is not necessarily an asset, if you are only interested in blocking one or two categories.

Feature 21: Option to Warn vs. Block

Giving users an option to decide whether to see a site is something more filters will offer in the future.

Feature 22: Edit Denial Message

This is usually an HTML file that can be customized to provide information about what is blocked, why it is blocked, and whom to contact for site reconsideration.

Feature 23: PICS Support

Though most vendors indicated they thought PICS was not yet a serious feature, they were all concerned about supporting it, due to many customer enquiries.

Feature 24: Password Override

This means that a privileged user, such as a librarian, can override a block by entering a password (sometimes for a preset length of time).

Feature 25: Monitor vs. Block

Best combined with good reporting capabilities breaking down blocks and accesses by categories, this feature is very useful for identifying if you have a problem in the first place.

Feature 26: Email Link for Reconsiderations

Most filters have an email address dedicated to reconsiderations. Sometimes this address is built into the default denial message.

Feature 27: Multiple Privilege Levels
Feature 28: Remote Administration
Feature 29: Reporting Capabilities

These features are more common in server-based products.

FILTER FEATURES

	Feature	Version
1	Vendor-supplied site list	
2	# of staff maintaining list	
3	View Site List	
4	Edit Site List	
5	Site List update frequency	
6	Automated list download	
7	Support Third-Party Lists	
8	Local access/deny lists	
9	Keyword filtering	
10	Can disable keyword filtering	
11	Block to file level	
12	Block by protocol	
13	Block by time of day	
14	Host resolves to IP	
15	Support time-outs	
16	Configure by IP address	
17	Configure by user ID	
18	Support patron barcodes	
19	Vendor-defined categories	
20	Block or enable by categories	

21	Option to warn vs. block	
22	Edit denial message	
23	PICS support	
24	Password override	
25	Monitor vs. block	
26	Email link for reconsiderations	
27	Multiple privilege levels	
28	Remote administration	
29	Reporting capabilities	

BESS

Summary

Bess is really two products. One is a shared proxy server, where the subscriber's Internet requests are passed through a server located at the company, and the other solution is a dedicated server, which can be on-site or remote. Technical performance, as with most proxy servers, was so good it was a non-issue, and features such as remote administration, clear if rudimentary reporting, and configurable denial pages are welcome. At the moment, most of the configuration of the dedicated server is done by the company on user request; this is a nuisance. However, N2H2 says the next version, projected in early 1998, will include more local control. The shared proxy server limits the customer to the Bess default settings, including keyword blocking, though N2H2 representatives said they were considering establishing a specially-configured shared proxy server for library customers. In either version, support for more library-oriented resource allocation and administrative features would be welcome, and is anticipated as Bess expands beyond its relatively homogeneous K-12 clientele.

Blocking

Bess blocks http through its server, and if the service selected is the locally installed "proxy in a box," N2H2 will also configure a packet filter at the router level to block irc and Usenet.

Bess, like all filters, performs better with keyword blocking disabled, though the standard configuration is with it enabled. It stumbled on simple terms such as "pornography," "vagina," "sex," "penis" (though not "penile") and "babes."

In the dedicated version, forcing the administrator to request enabling or disabling categories limits the ability to dynamically evaluate or configure Bess. The inability to select categories at all in the shared product, including disabling keyword filtering, makes this version of questionable use in a library setting.

Overall, in TIFAP and in my own testing, nearly every pornographic site was blocked, and there seemed to be very little friendly fire. Bess did an outstanding job with question 4L, related to AIDS and fisting; it retrieved a very useful site and blocked individual links from this page that were pornographic. "Very nicely executed," as the tester remarked. Bess also competently blocked IP addresses for pornographic sites.

With keyword blocking disabled but all categories enabled, Bess blocked several sites that were not pornographic. One was a site discussing X-rated videos, though not providing any graphic representation; another was a page with a very clear illustration of the vaginal disease, trichomaniasis, which, after a review request, the company later decided to unblock. Again, this illustrates the need for local control of categories—and for librarians to pay attention to what the filter is doing.

In the dedicated version, Bess supports local access/deny lists, and as described below, makes them very easy to maintain.

User/Workstation Configuration

Bess can be enabled or disabled for individual workstations on the network (IP configuration), but it does not yet support different workstations with different categories.

Resource Allocation

Again, those features available must be requested from N2H2 staff at present.

Privilege Levels and Password Override

Bess allows the administrator to create user accounts with limited privileges, including the ability to override sites for predetermined period.

Denial Pages and User Feedback

Bess sets an excellent example in this area. A standard Bess graphic always appears on the bottom of Web pages when Bess is enabled for that workstation, and the standard denial message includes links to recommend site reconsideration and to the password override.

In the dedicated version, both the standard page footer and the denial page can be customized by the adminstrator.

Administration, Reporting, and Tech Support

Remote administration and 24 x 7 technical support, promptly rendered by knowledgeable personnel, are features to note.

BESS

Bullets • are features vendors said they would support on market demand. Information *in italics* was supplied by the vendor.

Company and Address
N2H2
http://www.n2h2.com
info@n2h2.com
800–971–2622

Versions

Client: none

Server:
Bess offers two types of proxy server services: shared and dedicated. The shared proxy server is located at the company's computer site. The dedicated proxy server can be located at the library or at the company's computer site.

Pricing examples:
$500 set-up plus $3 per-workstation monthly license
$4,000 for server plus $1 per workstation monthly license

Warranty:
See license agreement

Technical Support:
24 hours a day/7 days a week telephone and online support

BESS

Feature	Shared	Dedicated
Vendor-supplied site list	Yes	Yes
# of staff maintaining list	Unknown	Unknown
View Site List	No	No
Edit Site List	No	No
Site List update frequency	Daily	Daily
Automated list download	N/A	Yes
Support Third-Party Lists	Yes	Yes
Local access/deny lists	Yes	Yes
Keyword filtering	Yes	Yes
Can disable keyword filtering[1]	No	Yes
Block to file level	Yes	Yes
Block by protocol[2]	Yes	Yes
Block by time of day	No	Note 1
Host resolves to IP	Yes	Yes
Support time-outs•	No	Planned
Configure by IP address[3]	Limited	Soon
Configure by user ID•	No	No
Support patron barcodes•	No	No
Vendor-defined categories	Yes	Yes
Block or enable by categories•	No	Yes
Option to warn vs. block•	No	No
Edit denial message	No	Yes
PICS support•	No	No
Password override	Yes	Yes
Monitor vs. block	Yes	Yes
Email link for reconsiderations	Yes	Yes
Multiple privilege levels	No	Yes
Remote administration	Yes	Yes
Reporting capabilities	No	Yes

1. By request, at present.
2. Bess blocks http; with on-site server, N2H2 provides packet filter to block irc and nntp
3. Only "blocked" or "clear-channel"

CYBERSITTER

Summary

Not recommended. Poor software performance, keyword blocking cannot be disabled, it lacks a denial message and obliterates unobjectionable words in any resident program; yet in evaluation, it was easy to circumvent well-known pornographic sites if the IP number of the blocked host was known. While the latest version allows category configuration, it does not lift this product from the bottom of the heap. Note: Solid Oak Software is being sued for blocking sites critical of Cybersitter.

Versions

Cybersitter97, a client program. TIFAP tested the prior version; I downloaded and reassessed the new version.

Blocking

When people talk about filtering software blocking terms such as "breast," they are probably referring to this product. Cybersitter, which relies heavily on keyword blocking—you cannot disable this feature—claims it "actually looks at how the word or phrase is used in context." As one TIFAP tester reported, "nothing could be further from the truth." The classic example is the Frost poem, *Stopping by Woods on a Snowy Evening*, where the word "queer" is obliterated. (Cybersitter either leaves blanks or runs words together in its "contextual" filtering; as the tester commented, "I am not comfortable with a program that advertises it is 'working silently in the background'.") Cybersitter, she continued, has a "dangerous inconsistency"; she was able to access marijuana-growing guides but was denied access to a news article about legislating "pot." In one search, the terms "lesbian" and "your penis" were blanked out, but "vagina" was not. A keyword search for NAMBLA was blocked; directly typing in the URL was not. These were not isolated experiences but persistent performance issues with Cybersitter. I found, in addition, that it was painfully easy to bypass Cybersitter by inputting the IP addresses of host names for pornographic sites.

Cybersitter not only obliterates "bad" words on Web pages; every other Windows application will be scrubbed of the "offending" words (which made it difficult for the testers to email their forms with examples)—telnet sessions, OCLC searches, you name it. A colleague once emailed me a question about buttons; every instance of the character string "butt" was removed from the message.

Perhaps not surprisingly, Cybersitter supports local deny lists, but not local access lists.

User/Workstation Configuration

Cybersitter is designed for single-workstation use, presumably in a home setting.

Performance Issues

Plenteous. While I have encouraged you to test filters, whenever possible, I will warn you again: don't install this program on a critical computer. Testers reported numerous erratic Winsock (Windows Internet access) problems immediately after installation—and after deinstallation; it does not do a clean uninstall (I know this the hard way; it's still filtering words on my computer at work). At home, after evaluating it, I quickly uninstalled it because I suddenly developed "illegal operation" messages in programs that had given me no problem before. Some of these problems did not go away afterwards.

Resource Allocation

You can also block ftp, nntp and irc, and it does support SafeSurf and RSACI PICS levels.

Privilege Levels and Password Override

Cybersitter includes a password override for using the Internet without obstruction.

Denial Pages and User Feedback

The concept of a denial page is antithetical to a product that boasts of "working silently in the background." Cybersitter has an email address for site reconsiderations, though it is not linked from a form or otherwise automated for quick input.

Administration, Reporting, and Tech Support

Cybersitter has reporting capabilities, designed to monitor the user's use.

CYBERSITTER

Company and Address
Solid Oak Software
http://www.solidoak.com
PO Box 6826
Santa Barbara, California 93160
800–388–2761

Versions:

Client: Windows 95, NT

Server: None

Pricing examples:
$34.95

Warranty:
Unknown

Technical Support:
Telephone and email

CYBERSITTER

Feature	Client
Vendor-supplied site list	Yes
# of staff maintaining list	Unk
View Site List	No
Edit Site List	No
Site List update frequency	Wkly
Automated list download	Yes
Support Third-Party Lists	Yes
Local access/deny lists[1]	Note 1
Keyword filtering	Yes
Can disable keyword filtering	No
Block to file level	Yes
Block by protocol[2]	Yes
Block by time of day	No
Host resolves to IP	No
Support time-outs[3]	No
Configure by IP address	N/A
Configure by user ID	N/A
Support patron barcodes	No
Vendor-defined categories	6
Block or enable by categories	Yes
Option to warn vs. block	No
Edit denial message	No
PICS support	Yes
Password override	Yes
Monitor vs. block	Yes
Email link for reconsiderations	Yes
Multiple privilege levels	No
Remote administration	No
Reporting capabilities	Yes

1. Supports deny lists but not access lists
2. http, nntp, ftp, irc
3. Solid Oak sells a separate product that offers

I-GEAR

Summary

URLabs, a company with Unix and K-12 heritage, is rapidly redefining its server-based filter products for two brave new worlds: Microsoft and libraries. (The product URLabs sells is actually composed of several similarly-named components—I-Gear, I-Power-Admin, I-Guard, I-Visor, and I-Proxy—but I will refer to them collectively as "I-Gear.") The Unix product (the only one available at press time) demonstrated powerful control over user access privileges, by user as well as by workstation, and supported some key resource-allocation features, but lacked a configurable denial message. A couple of blocks showed that this product is still in rapid development. Remote administration, a responsive sales division, and superb user and workstation configuration round out a very interesting product.

Blocking

With keyword blocking disabled, and categories tuned to adult, I-Gear performed competently if imperfectly in TIFAP URL testing. With a weekend of dedicated access to the demonstration server, I reviewed additional sites and found that I-Gear continued to include the entire Yahoo Gay and Lesbian directory in its "adult" category. By I-Gear's own definition that site would be labeled "mature," not "adult." The company said it would fix this error, which I attribute to the haste with which I-Gear is repositioning itself for information-robust customers.

I-Gear competently blocked the IP addresses of several pornographic sites, and offers the optional capability to block unresolved IP addresses (directed towards fly-by-night pornography/child sex servers).

URLabs sincerely believes in, and heavily touts, the capability of its keyword blocking—excuse me, "Dynamic Document Review." The most significant feature about DDR is that it can be disabled. It is true that DDR employs elaborate keyword algorithms, and that it performs better than, for example, Cybersitter. Yet in TIFAP, with DDR enabled, we still found I-Gear blocked fairly obvious pages ("cockfighting," "pussycat"), and the justifications for why this happened (little calculation errors, since fixed; interference with the demonstration database) rang hollow to our skeptical librarian ears.

URLab's absolute faith in DDR is cracking a little; they admitted that they are "swiftly migrating to a 100% human-reviewed database."

Local Access/Deny Lists

I-Gear capably supports extensive configuration of local access/deny lists and local categories. Not only can you use local lists to override access and deny capabilities, you can shuffle information from category to category (note, this is not direct editing of the lists, but a "tagging" at your end). There are three switches for categories: allow, deny, and none—a very good feature if you are in the middle of building a special list. If you override a blocked search, you can then elect to add it to a local list.

User/Workstation Configuration Privilege Levels and Password Override

I-Gear is one of the few products to allow very specific levels of access by workstation or user ID, which can in turn be associated with groups for better management. Another feature lets you read in a list of user IDS from another source (such as exported from an OPAC), and there is no reason these could not be barcode numbers, which patrons could key in by hand. Levels of access can be tuned very specifically to the local environment, and there is a password override which expires at a preset time.

Resource Allocation

I-Gear supports time blocks and disabling protocols (the latter at the packet filter level, like most server products). I-Gear has two truly nifty patron-privacy features: both the browser history and the bookmarks are linked to the log-in session, meaning they disappear on log-out.

Denial Pages and User Feedback

The denial page cannot be edited, and might be meaningless—if not misleading—to the end-user. The phrase "forbidden," which it opens with, is usually associated with Web pages that have incorrect permissions. Links to administrative overrides and email feedback, while welcome, do not compensate for the ability to customize the denial page.

Administration, Reporting, and Tech Support

Reporting was rudimentary, though it does display denials by category; currently you cannot sort lists by criteria, though that feature is planned for the future.

I-GEAR

Bullets • are features vendors said they would support on market demand. Information *in italics* was supplied by the vendor.

Company and Address
http://www.urlabs.com
information@urlabs.com
303 Butler Farm Road, Suite 106
Hampton, VA 23666–1568 USA
757–865–0810

Versions: 2.6 at writing

Client: none

Server:
Windows NT plug-in for MS proxy (available early October; not available for evaluation for this book)
Unix (Sun/Solaris 2.5 only)

Pricing examples:
Windows NT/ MS Proxy:
$2685 for 50 simultaneous users, based on:
I-Gear 50–license user pack $1195
Software and list updates $995
Technical Support $495
Unix: $3090 for the same package (the company says they give a better price on the NT version because the customer also has to buy the Microsoft Proxy Server)

Warranty:
See license agreement

Technical Support:
Free for 30 days; then fee-based—see pricing above for examples.

I-GEAR

Feature	NT	Unix
Vendor-supplied site list	*Yes*	Yes
# of staff maintaining list	*Unk*	*Unk*
View Site List	*No*	No
Edit Site List	*No*	No
Site List update frequency	*Wkly*	Wkly
Automated list download	Yes	*Yes*
Support Third-Party Lists•	*No*	No
Local access/deny lists	*Yes*	Yes
Keyword filtering	*Yes*	Yes
Can disable keyword filtering	*Yes*	Yes
Block to file level	*Yes*	Yes
Block by protocol[1]	*Yes*	Yes
Block by time of day	*Yes*	Yes
Host resolves to IP	*Yes*	Yes
Support time-outs•	*No*	No
Configure by IP address	*Yes*	Yes
Configure by user ID	*Yes*	Yes
Support patron barcodes•	*No*	No
Vendor-defined categories[2]	*Yes*	Yes
Block or enable by categories	*Yes*	Yes
Option to warn vs. block•	*No*	No
Edit denial message•	*No*	No
PICS support	*Soon*	*Soon*
Password override	*Yes*	Yes
Monitor vs. block	*Soon*	*Soon*
Email link for reconsiderations	*Yes*	Yes
Multiple privilege levels	*Yes*	Yes
Remote administration	*Yes*	Yes
Reporting capabilities	*Yes*	Yes

1. Unix: via packet filter. NT: http, ftp, gopher
2. Categories currently undergoing reorganization

THE LIBRARY CHANNEL
VERSION 2.02

Summary

The Library Channel, also known as TLC, markets itself as a selection tool—a way for libraries to offer organized collections links to a variety of preselected Internet resources, including other tools, such as online catalogs and software. However, TLC also includes filtering methods common to other products in this book. Because TLC is a somewhat different tool than any other described in this book, this discussion will have different emphases than the other product discussions; thus there is no features table for this product.

System Requirements and Performance Issues

TLC 2.02 is client software that requires Windows 95 or NT, Microsoft Explorer 3.02 or higher, at least 32 megabytes of RAM, and a video card capable of displaying high color (65,000 colors). Windows 95 must be set to use small fonts.

TLC 2.02 installed very easily. For the rest of the testing period, the software worked without incident and did not interfere with any other applications.

Levels of administration are designed with an awareness of a typical public library environment. A system administrator can control all TLC settings, and other administrators can have levels of access that include adding or deleting information in the database and overriding TLC settings temporarily. A patron login is specifically configured for limited, search-only access, and a kiosk mode is designed to make TLC the boot-up shell, eliminating the Windows 95 taskbar (the Kiosk mode is not available for NT).

Collection Capabilities: CyberShelves

Off the shelf, TLC organizes itself into 18 "Worlds" of information, but it can be organized around other groups of topics and subtopics. A final level of organization is the "Cybershelves," Web pages with 9 large squares which can be linked to more levels, or to individual URLs.

Authorized staff add URLs to TLC via the Resource Linker. This tool, similar to one in I-Gear, allows the librarian to locate a resource and add it to the database. This procedure is very smooth, similar to the same process in I-Gear; the librarian clicks the Paste Button, and the URL enters the field. After adding the URL, the librarian assigns this resource a title and some keywords, and designates domain range and domain surfing (discussed below). The procedure for adding an application such as a game or CD-ROM is equally simple.

Blocking Capabilities: URL Bar, Denial Lists, Domain Surfing, and Domain Range

TLC includes several options for controlling whether Internet content outside the TLC database is accessible to patrons. TLC includes a denial list capability, called the De-Selection List. Patron activity can be further restricted through disabling the URL Bar (an open field for typing in URLs, similar to a browser's "Location" field).

Domain Surfing is another TLC blocking feature. With this feature enabled, the user can only navigate Web links and content "under the specified domain name." If you went to the Hayes Bolt site, as TIFAP testers did when answering a question about screw manufacturing, you would be able to access http://www.hayes.com. However, you would not be able to access its recommended links, such as that delightfully useless site, The Amazing Fish Cam, at http://www.netscape.com/fishcam/. Domain Surfing can be enabled globally or on a site-by-site basis.

Domain Range is a limiting feature applied to individual URLs. Surfing can be limited to one or more domains beyond the domain the user links to from the Topic or CyberShelf. In this case, if TLC included a link to http://www.hayes.com, and the Domain Range was set to 1, the user could go to The Amazing Fish Cam, but not beyond this domain. If the Domain Range was 2, the user could go one domain beyond the Fish Cam, then return back to TLC through http://www.hayes.com.

Denial Page

TLC builds in a capability for a denial page. URLs labeled as "Wrong" in the Deselection List can be redirected to the "Right" URL. TLC provides a default Web page for the "Right" URL, but the library can configure this page as required.

Search Capabilities

TLC is intended to be a searchable database of preselected links, and as such, require that its search capabilities be assessed. It is here that TLC seriously founders.

First, the indexing is very limited. The version I tested, 2.02, only allowed me to search by title, URL, and keywords. "No multiple terms, no tracings, no discernable hierarchy," as one tester commented. I believe what is driving this very minimal indexing is the time-intensive nature of collecting these links, since TLC currently outsources this work to one of its customers. However, anyone familiar with either the richness of MARC cataloging or the full-text freedom of searching the Internet will understand that searching such a limited catalog will not meet user needs for information retrieval. Terms a user might not approach a librarian for assistance with—including herpes, trich, and penis—return 1 or no results. A smaller, more easily repaired problem is the message that appears when no results occur: "search found nothing." This message (not to be confused with the "Right" message, discussed above) should indicate that the information probably exists, but the user can't get there without seeking assistance.

TLC includes many quality sites, and it is possible to answer many questions in TLC through drill-down, that is, by stepping down from larger to smaller categories and then following appropriate links. The TIFAP testers (of which I was one) were able to answer all questions this way, no doubt due to our library background. The questions are whether librarians want to search this way, and whether users are able to. 94% of the time, TIFAP testers used keyword searching to answer a question, even though a number of structured directories capable of drill-down, such as Yahoo, are available on the Internet. The need to structure information very carefully should not be confused with the ability or desire to search that way.

This leads to the last conundrum of TLC. You can provide access to search engines and let users follow or launch links to their heart's desire; or TLC can be all or partially "locked down," to quote another TIFAP tester, to filter access to information not intentionally added to the TLC database. If you do the former, then why not just create a really solid library Website, perhaps with a simple search engine, and let users follow their own interests? If you do the latter, to quote a tester, "you have something, but you don't have the Web…it's not the whole enchilada." This product may have its niche, and some people are buying it; as with other products, I recommend you test it and find out for yourself.

THE LIBRARY CHANNEL

Company and Address
Vimpact, Inc.
http://www.vimpact.net
vimpact@infinet.com
612 North Park Street
Columbus Ohio, 43215
614–224–7383

Versions:

Client: Version 2.02 Windows 95, NT (Requires Microsoft Explorer 3.02 or higher)

Server:
Not available

Pricing examples:
10 "seats" (workstations) plus updates are $3600. 100 seats plus updates are $17,600.

Warranty:
Unknown

Technical Support:
Unknown

NET NANNY

Summary

To paraphrase one TIFAP volunteer, Net Nanny is a program I wanted to like. It's a small client, keyword blocking can be disabled, you can view and edit the site lists, and it includes the elusive warn-vs.-block feature. However, in addition to very few resource allocation tools, the scanty and outdated site lists make this product unusable in a library environment unless you are willing to load and manage a third-party list. Even then, it is so short on features that Net Nanny is not a first choice among clients.

Blocking

Net Nanny doesn't exactly rely on keyword blocking—there are only 11 keywords on its list, which can be easily disabled. You will want to disable these keywords, because they interfere with routine searching of any page that contains, as one TIFAP volunteer found, "sex," "drugs," and "bomb." The AKC site for Dachshunds had the word "sex" obliterated, though it was in a non-prurient context; pharmaceutical sites and press releases easily fall victim to this very simple blocking routine.

On the other hand, there are six site lists that come with Net Nanny; they are not only limited and uncategorized, but seriously dated. One volunteer concatenated the lists into one text file; it only measured 152KB (or about one-tenth of a floppy disk). These lists are in no apparent order, which makes it difficult to know what the intent of any particular group of URLs is for, let alone disable them. A simple visual scan of the lists revealed obsolete URLs, such as this one from the early Yahoo Website: http://akebono. standard.edu/yahoo/Art/Erotica/Pictures.

Sure enough, I was able to launch six-month-old pornography URLs with no problem. Even keyword blocking did not prevent me from drilling down two pages into the sexually explicit http:// www.creampie.com.

Net Nanny supports access and denial lists (though has very little information on how they should be configured or imported). The nicest touch in Net Nanny is that the administrator can select four different actions when a blocked site is reached:

1. Mask words on screen
2. Log the hit
3. Give warning message
4. Shut down the program

Performance Issues

Net Nanny installed relatively smoothly, but shut down Word when I pasted two URLs for pornography sites into an open Word document (I could have overridden Net Nanny, but I could not remember my new password in time). I removed the programs from the list of affected tools, but this is not a good feature. If they were in the list before installation, all the worse for Net Nanny; if a program wants to perform *literarius interruptus*, it should warn me before it enables this feature.

Resource Allocation

Net Nanny does not allow time blocking, time-outs, protocol blocking or similar allocation.

User/Workstation Configuration
Privilege Levels and Password Override

Net Nanny allows users to be configured to access specific lists (again, I don't know how you would know which lists to use). There is an administrative override, but no special category for users in between administrators and end users. For each user the administrator can decide whether the program should shut down or if the user can enter a password to override the shut-down and continue searching (though not access the blocked site).

Denial Pages and User Feedback

Denial pages cannot be configured, and the warning is simply "AC-CESS DENIED, This is an unauthorized Internet site"—no explanation of what is blocked, why it is unauthorized, or what to do if you disagree with the block. Since Net Nanny emphasizes local configuration, it isn't surprising that requests for reconsideration of blocked or unblocked sites is not addressed.

Administration, Reporting, and Tech Support

Net Nanny logs all hits, though does not say why something is blocked. I have had quick responses from emailing technical support.

NET NANNY

Company and Address
http://www.netnanny.com
netnanny@netnanny.com.
Net Nanny Software International Inc.
Suite 108 - 525 Seymour Street
Vancouver, B.C. Canada, V6B 3H7
Phone : 1–800–340–7177
Fax : (604)-662–8525

Version Discussed: 3.1

Client: Windows 3*, 95

Server: None

Pricing examples:
1 license: $26.95
20–license pack: $199.95

Warranty:
Unknown

Technical Support:
Phone: voice (604) 662–8522
         fax: (604) 662–8525
email: NNsupport@netnanny.com

NET NANNY

Feature	Client
Vendor-supplied site list	Yes
# of staff maintaining list	Unk
View Site List	Yes
Edit Site List	Yes
Site List update frequency	biwkly
Automated list download	No
Support Third-Party Lists	Yes
Local access/deny lists	Yes
Keyword filtering	Yes
Can disable keyword filtering	Yes
Block to file level	Yes
Block by protocol[1]	Yes
Block by time of day	No
Host resolves to IP[2]	No
Support time-outs	No
Configure by IP address	N/A
Configure by user ID[3]	Yes
Support patron barcodes	No
Vendor-defined categories	No
Block or enable by categories	N/A
Option to warn vs. block	Yes
Edit denial message	No
PICS support	No
Password override	Yes
Monitor vs. block	Yes
Email link for reconsiderations	Yes
Multiple privilege levels	No
Remote administration	No
Reporting capabilities	Yes

1. http, ftp, irc, smtp, nntp, irc
2. Supports this feature, but was easily defeated
3. Usernames with passwords

NET SHEPHERD

Summary

Net Shepherd is a client product that relies on its own PICS rating system, based on age levels, and its own label bureau. It suffers from the same limitations of other selection-oriented tools: its site list is too limited. If Net Shepherd is configured so unrated sites are accessible, it lets through far too many sites. Lack of compatibility with other PICS-based tools, limited resource-allocation tools and the inability to shut down Net Shepherd without uninstalling are also significant problems.

Version Comments

Net Shepherd is available for Windows 3.1 and Windows 95. At press, the Net Shepherd Website noted that Net Shepherd was not compatible with Netscape Communicator 4.0 or Explorer 4.0, but it installed and worked smoothly with Explorer 3.0.

Blocking

Net Shepherd performed very poorly in TIFAP in terms of how much it blocked, so I bought, installed and retested it to see what was going on. Net Shepherd does not rely on keyword blocking, but it does rely on its own proprietary PICS label bureau, created by its company and by volunteer efforts and organized around age levels (general, child, pre-teen, teen, adult, and objectionable).

Like other access-oriented tools, such as The Library Channel, Net Shepherd's reliance on a selection-oriented technology creates an interesting conundrum. As with other PICS-enabled tools (for example, Cyber Patrol and Explorer), you can choose whether or not unrated sites can be accessed by users (and you can select this by user, as well). If you configure Net Shepherd so it cannot access unrated sites, a lot will be blocked. It blocked safe sex information, AIDS information, and even some of the competing products listed in this book. Before you get paranoid, though, I used a second account I had established, where unrated sites could be accessed, and verified that none of these sites were in the Net Shepherd database. Unfortunately, at these settings, I was able to get into about half the pornography sites I attempted. Net Shepherd, unlike Library Channel, doesn't have the added value of organizing information. Finally, I was able to circumvent the Net Shepherd database several times by putting in the IP address of a host which Net Shepherd blocked.

Resource Allocation

Net Shepherd does not have any tools for managing access by time, time-outs, warn-vs.-block, or monitor-vs.-block.

User/Workstation Configuration Privilege Levels and Password Override

Net Shepherd allows the administrator to create an infinite number of accounts, associated with age levels, administrative privilege, protocol access (for irc and Usenet), and access to unrated sites. Because Net Shepherd is a client product, this feature is limited to each workstation.

Net Shepherd does not have a password override *per se*; the administrator must log in (and then remember to log out).

Denial Pages and User Feedback

The denial message is the same whether the site was blocked at that level or whether it is unrated. This message, which cannot be edited, is:

Sorry! The page you've requested has a rating that does not match the access level of your Net Shepherd account. If you think you've reached this message in error, please contact your Net Shepherd Administrator.

Due to the number of unrated sites, this results in a very misleading picture of the information universe.

Software Issues

The only way to shut down Net Shepherd is to uninstall it. This is supposed to make Net Shepherd harder to disable; however, other products handle this more elegantly through their administrative functions.

Administration, Reporting, and Tech Support

Administration is limited to setting access levels. There are no reporting features in Net Shepherd.

NET SHEPHERD

Company and Address
http://www.shepherd.net
info@netshepherd.com
Net Shepherd Inc.
1250, 815 - 8th Avenue SW
Calgary, Alberta Canada T2P 3P2
(403) 205–6677

Versions: 2.0 at time of press

Client: Windows 3.1, 95

Server: Not available

Pricing examples:
$12.00 for year includes client software and access to Net Shepherd database

Warranty:
Unknown

Technical Support:
Online help files and email assistance

NET SHEPHERD

Feature	Client
Vendor-supplied site list	Yes
# of staff maintaining list	Unk
View Site List	No
Edit Site List	No
Site List update frequency	Unk
Automated list download	N/A
Support Third-Party Lists[1]	No
Local access/deny lists	Yes
Keyword filtering	No
Can disable keyword filtering	N/A
Block to file level	Yes
Block by protocol[2]	Yes
Block by time of day	No
Host resolves to IP	No
Support time-outs	No
Configure by IP address	N/A
Configure by user ID	Yes
Support patron barcodes	No
Vendor-defined categories	Yes
Block or enable by categories	Yes
Option to warn vs. block	No
Edit denial message	No
PICS support	Limited
Password override	Note 2
Monitor vs. block	No
Email link for reconsiderations[3]	Note 3
Multiple privilege levels	Yes
Remote administration	No
Reporting capabilities	No

1. Net Shepherd does not support other PICS ratings
2. http, nntp, irc
3. Local ratings can be submitted to Net Shepherd

SMART FILTER

Summary

Smart Filter is a server-based product that was not only evaluated in TIFAP but was installed and examined by a TIFAP volunteer who is a systems librarian. Smart Filter has good local access/deny list capabilities, and supports monitor-vs.-block as well as several resource allocation features. Smart Filter supports multiple privilege levels but limits the password override to the administrator. Technical support personnel were hard to reach. Solid software performance but a small number of questionable blocks make this a product to look at, but try before you buy.

Blocking

Smart Filter was only assessed in the URL-testing phase of TIFAP; 26 of its categories were disabled and only Sex was enabled for blocking. Of 112 URLs, Smart Filter blocked 12, and of these, 7 appeared to be miscategorized. For example, three sites promoting marijuana use, three sites with (non-prurient) gay-related information and a safe-sex site were blocked; the denial message indicated these were all blocked in the "sex" category, which appears to be inaccurate. As one tester commented, "It's a mystery to me why this site was blocked. I've tried, and I can't find any 'sex'." Perhaps better granularity in the sexuality categories and more attention to detail would help improve this product's blocking capabilities.

Like several other filters, Smart Filter blocked a non-prurient subdirectory of a Website whose top-level files were pornographic. This appears to be a technical issue, though this does not obviate the problem.

While Smart Filter offers keyword blocking capability for search engine arguments, it does not provide a list of keywords or emphasize this feature, which can be disabled. Automated weekly list downloads help keep the site lists current.

Smart Filter supports local access/deny lists, and a company representative told me that a "warn-vs.-block" feature was imminent (the Unix version of their product already offers this).

User/Workstation Configuration

At writing, Smart Filter could not support multiple configurations; a workstation is either set to Smart Filter settings or "clear channel," in the jargon of proxy-server vendors, though this was due to change shortly, according to company representatives, who added that we should watch for their support for user IDs.

Resource Allocation

Smart Filter blocks by protocol and by time of day; the company expressed interest in time-outs.

Privilege Levels and Password Override

Smart Filter has two privilege levels: the administrator and a sub-administrator. However, the sub-administrator cannot override blocked sites. Librarians at the "front desk" would have to ask the administrator to unblock sites or immediately add these sites to the access lists, which would interrupt information services.

Denial Pages and User Feedback

Smart Filter allows full editing of its denial message. The default message usefully reports the category the site was blocked in, such as "sex." Smart Filter reviews sites for reconsideration, though my experience with technical support—shared by two other librarians I communicate with—suggests that it would be important to carbon-copy reconsideration requests to the library staff.

Reporting and Tech Support

The manual, available online, is cursory. Technical support was, as noted, aggravatingly difficult to track down. The vendor said remote administration was possible "if you have access to the server."

Reporting capabilities offer real-time monitoring by IP address, as well as daily management reports. In the reports, however, IP addresses are not resolved to alphanumeric host names, which also detracts somewhat from the otherwise excellent feature to monitor (rather than simply block) network traffic by category. Much to their credit, company representatives encouraged me to use the monitoring tool to determine if "there really is a problem, and where it is." Reports can provide hits by time of day, filetype and number of hits per category.

SMART FILTER (FORMERLY WEBTRACK)

Bullets • are features vendors said they would support on market demand. Information *in italics* was supplied by the vendor.

Address:
info@smartfilter.com
http://www.smartfilter.com
Secure Computing Corporation
Web Tools Division
1100 5th Avenue South, Suite 307
Naples, FL 34102
800–379–4944

Versions:

Client: None

Server-based:
Standalone proxy for NT or Unix; plug-in proxy server for a variety of platforms and products, including CSM Proxy Plus, Netcache Proxy Server, Sidewinder Firewall, Borderware, Checkpoint, and more. Contact company for additional versions and custom plug-ins.

Pricing examples:
Standalone proxy:
$2,000 50–user license; $4,000 250–user license; $6,000 unlimited users.

Warranty:
30–day free download; see license agreement for warranty.

Technical Support:
Telephone support, 8 a.m. - 9 p.m. PDT, plus online support

SMART FILTER

Feature	Stand-alone	Plug-In
Vendor-supplied site list	Yes	Yes
# of staff maintaining list	12	12
View Site List	No	No
Edit Site List	No	No
Site List update frequency	Wkly	Wkly
Automated list download	Yes	Yes
Support Third-Party Lists	No	No
Local access/deny lists	Yes	Yes
Keyword filtering	Yes	Yes
Can disable keyword filtering	Yes	Yes
Block to file level	Yes	Yes
Block by protocol[1]	Yes	Yes
Block by time of day	Yes	Yes
Host resolves to IP	Yes	Yes
Support time-outs	No	No
Configure by IP address[2]	Limited	Limited
Configure by user ID	Soon	Soon
Support patron barcodes•	No	No
Vendor-defined categories	27	27
Block or enable by categories	Yes	Yes
Option to warn vs. block	Soon	Soon
Edit denial message	Yes	Yes
PICS support	Soon	Soon
Password override	No	No
Monitor vs. block	No	No
Email link for reconsiderations	Yes	Yes
Multiple privilege levels	Yes	Yes
Remote administration	Yes	Note[3]
Reporting capabilities	Yes	Yes

---

1. Firewall: http; NT also ftp, nntp and gopher
2. Only blocked vs. clear-channel
3. Depends on the version and platform

SURFWATCH

Summary

The client version was the only one evaluated for this book; Surfwatch also comes in server-based products that appear to be completely different in their functionality. However, the client version is not suitable in a library setting. Keyword blocking cannot be disabled, and the Surfwatch client lacks resource-allocation features and administrative management. Surfwatch functioned unobtrusively and uninstalled very neatly.

Blocking

Keyword blocking cannot be disabled (though Surfwatch said this could be done on request, I doubt custom programming would be cost-effective on a per-client basis), and this is a serious deficiency. While you can indeed search for breast cancer and chicken breasts, other terms have the presumption of prurience. Simple terms such as "penis" and "vaginal" are automatically blocked if you enter them in a search engine (though "penile" was not blocked). While some of the better-known sites had been added to Surfwatch's access list, because it appears to block keywords in URL titles and in search engine searches, it still blocked the useful safe-sex guide, http://www.utopia-asia.com/safe.htm, and the excellent guide for sexual activity for the disabled, http://www.curbcut.com/Sex.html.

Set only to the sexually-explicit category, I had the sense that Surfwatch was laboring to provide decent information, but could not escape the shadow of keyword blocking. The Dachshund-L home page displayed just fine, as did the Hooters home page. However, Surfwatch blocked two sites that were not sexually explicit: the NAMBLA home page and a site discussing, but not displaying, pornography.

Add/deny is easy to use, though only one list can be created (each item is individually defined as add or deny). You can also choose to install custom filters—subsets of the Surfwatch database, so that only one type of information is ever blocked.

Surfwatch blocked the Websites of several pornographic sites when I entered their IP addresses.

The Yahooligans feature sounds promising. Yahooligans is a re-source created by Yahoo for children. The Surfwatch feature limits all searching to the http://www.yahooligans.com domain and the links it has selected.

I found that the Yahooligans setting in Surfwatch had a distinct flavor (or lack of it, depending on your point of view). Searches for terms such as "birth control," "contraceptive," "racism," "geno-cide," "french occupation," and "Oscar Wilde" came up with the message, "No Yahooligans! Site Matches." These would all be fruit-ful searches in the "adult" Yahoo (though the search for "french occupation" bounced to Alta Vista, which Yahooligans also doesn't do).

The extremely helpful Surfwatch representatives explained that Yahooligans was for "casual use" of the "7–12 crowd," and was not intended for research. Like Maurice Chevalier and the French Occupation, it's hard to determine where the real fault lies, but some-how, Surfwatch and Yahoo created a resource that paints a world far more sanitized (and dull) than most children live in. Do chil-dren really need to wait until puberty to find out that life has many sides to it?

Resource Allocation

Surfwatch does not offer time blocks, time-outs or similar public-access tools. It will block Usenet and chat, as a combined resource. It will work in conjunction with a proxy server.

Privilege Levels and Password Override
User/Workstation Configuration

The Surfwatch client is designed for one setting, with an adminis-trative override.

Denial Pages and User Feedback

The Surfwatch denial page cannot be edited. It states only, "Blocked by Surfwatch," without citing what was blocked or providing in-formation about submitting requests for reconsideration.

The company is very responsive to reconsideration requests, sometimes responding the same day, and can be reached for reconsiderations by email.

Reporting and Tech Support

The Surfwatch client has no reporting capabilities. Its technical support is friendly and responsive.

SURFWATCH

Bullets • are features vendors said they would support on market demand

Company and Address
http://www.surfwatch.com
sales@surfwatch.com
Surfwatch Software, Inc.
Los Altos, CA 94022
800–458–6600

Versions:

Client:
Windows 3.x, 95, Macintosh

Server:
Microsoft Proxy, Oracle Proxy, Firewall
Standalone proxy server due out in spring 98

Pricing examples:

Client: Often bundled with other packages; under $30

Warranty:
Unknown

Technical Support:
Phone support: 8:30–5:30 p.m. PDT, Monday - Friday
Online support available

SURFWATCH

Feature	Client	MS Proxy	Firewall
Vendor-supplied site list	Yes	Yes	Yes
# of staff maintaining list	14	14	14
View Site List	No	No	No
Edit Site List	No	No	No
Site List update frequency	Daily	Daily	Daily
Automated list download	Yes	Yes	Yes
Support Third-Party Lists[1]	Note 1	Note 1	Note 1
Local access/deny lists	Yes	Yes	Yes
Keyword filtering	Yes	Yes	Yes
Can disable keyword filtering	Note 1	Note 1	Note1
Block to file level	Yes	Yes	Yes
Block by protocol[2]	Yes	Yes	Yes
Block by time of day	Soon	Soon	Soon
Host resolves to IP	Yes	Yes	Yes
Support time-outs	Soon	Soon	Soon
Configure by IP address	N/A	Soon	Yes
Configure by user ID	No	Soon	Yes
Support patron barcodes•	No	No	No
Vendor-defined categories	7	7	7
Block or enable by categories	Yes	Yes	Yes
Option to warn vs. block	Soon	Soon	Soon
Edit denial message	No	Yes	Note[3]
PICS support	Yes	Yes	Yes
Password override	Yes	No	No
Monitor vs. block	No	No	No
Email link for reconsiderations	Yes	Yes	Yes
Multiple privilege levels	No	Yes	Yes
Remote administration	No	No	Yes
Reporting capabilities	No	Yes	Yes

1. Surfwatch says this can be done on request
2. http, gopher, and ftp for all; client also nntp and irc
3. Controlled by firewall capabilities

WEBSENSE

Summary

Websense is a flexible NT-based product that has acquired some library customers, though its heritage is in the business environment, as some of the features it lacks betray. It did well at blocking and is reportedly easy to configure and maintain. Two strong features are its ability to monitor-vs.-block, and its good reporting. It lacks local password override capability, time-outs, configuration by workstation and support for user logins. Libraries that use it have commented to me on its unobtrusive and reliable performance. Technical support was prompt, knowledgeable, and concerned, and the documentation was well-written.

Blocking

In TIFAP, it was unclear whether more than two settings were enabled where Websense was tested, and the volunteer could not confirm the settings. However, an independent third party identified that the sites that caused concern were not blocked when only sex and chat were enabled for blocking. Beyond this question, Websense did a very good job of blocking pornography, including by IP address, and let through a wide variety of resources appropriate for library settings. One of the sites it blocked, however, was a discussion of X-Rated videos, not in itself prurient.

Two evaluators commented that Websense had weak performance in blocking chat sites. One evaluator said that half the Web-based chat sites in Yahoo could be accessed, even with chat enabled; a second confirmed that very little chat appeared to be blocked.

Websense has a technical problem with one Website, http://www.webcom.com. Due to a peculiarity of how this site supports its virtual servers, Websense blocks every site WebCom hosts, since one of the sites includes sexually-explicit information. The company said they were working on this problem and that it should be fixed by the next version.

One block I reported caused several meetings at Websense, due to the fact that a "good" resource was held hostage one directory below a pornography site. The technical support kept in touch with me, and explained the technical problems involved in enabling the subdirectory.

Resource Allocation

In addition to enabling or disabling protocols, Websense supports time blocks.

Privilege Levels and Password Override User/Workstation Configuration

Websense can only be enabled "on" or "off" (blocked or clear-channel) per workstation; it does not understand the concept of user IDs. The very clear documentation makes configuration appear easy; those who have set it up have confirmed this.

Websense also does not support password overrides in the sense of local users who can temporarily override blocks.

Denial Pages and User Feedback

The Websense denial page is completely configurable by the administrator. Websense has an email address for submitting requests for reconsideration.

Reporting and Tech Support

Websense not only supports monitor-vs.-block, but encourages using this feature as a way to observe network behavior before configuring categories. Reporting tracking is by category, date, destination, and workstation. Report output capabilities include summary reports by category, which can be output as text or as graph files, and reports by workstation.

The documentation, a single Acrobat file, is extensive and well-written; it even includes an index.

Technical support, as discussed above, was prompt, clear, and concerned with the quality of their response.

WEBSENSE

Bullets • are features vendors said they would support on market demand. Information *in italics* was supplied by the vendor.

Netpartners
Internet Solutions Inc.
http://www.websense.com
9210 Sky Park Court
1st Floor
San Diego, CA 92123
800–723–1166

Version at writing: 3.01

Pending version updates:
October 97: 3.1
January 98: 4.0

Versions

Client:
None

Server-based:
One version, which can work with:
Windows NT (standalone)
Netscape Proxy, Microsoft Proxy
Unix Firewall

Pricing Examples (subject to change and negotiation):
25 users $495
1,000 $4795
Unlimited $6995

Warranty
No; 30–day free trial.

Technical Support:
First 30 days of purchase

Documentation:
NT standalone 3.01 was clear and extensive.

WEBSENSE

Feature	Stand-Alone	NS/MSProxy	Firewall
Vendor-supplied site list	Yes	Yes	Yes
# of staff maintaining list	9	9	9
View Site List	No	No	No
Edit Site List	No	No	No
Site List update frequency	Daily	Daily	Daily
Automated list download	Yes	Yes	Yes
Support Third-Party Lists	No	No	No
Local access and deny lists	Yes	Yes	Yes
Keyword filtering	No	No	No
Can disable keyword filtering	N/A	N/A	N/A
Block to file level	Yes	Yes	Yes
Block by protocol[1]	Yes	Yes	Yes
Block by time of day	Yes	Yes	Yes
Reverse DNS lookups	Yes	Yes	Yes
Support time-outs	No•	No•	No•
Configure by IP address	Limited	Limited	Limited
Configure by user ID	Soon•	Yes•	Yes•
Support patron barcodes	No•	No•	No•
Vendor-defined categories	29	29	29
Block or enable by categories	Yes	Yes	Yes
Option to warn vs. block	No•	No•	No•
Edit denial message	Yes	Yes	Yes
PICS support	Soon	Soon	Soon
Password override	No	No	No
Monitor vs. block	Yes	Yes	Yes
Email link for reconsiderations	Yes	Yes	Yes
Multiple privilege levels	Yes	Yes	Yes
Remote administration	No	No	Yes
Reporting capabilities	Yes	Yes	Yes

---

1.   http, gopher, ftp, nntp, irc, telnet on NT versions; http on firewall

CYBER PATROL

Summary

Cyber Patrol comes in many versions. The client version is best known, and was evaluated for this book. The client installs with all settings fully enabled, and despite some recent improvements it is still clumsy to configure—and you *will* want to configure it. Reporting is limited, the message displayed to the user is uninformative and cannot be edited, and its resource allocation tools are designed more for home use. However, it performed better than the other clients evaluated for this book, due to its high configurability.

Blocking

In TIFAP, we looked at Cyber Patrol several ways: with all categories fully enabled, with categories enabled but keyword blocking disabled, and tweaked to minimal settings—blocking full nudity and sexual acts, with keyword blocking disabled (note, however, that the "Carlin 7" words can't be disabled). Only the minimal configuration performed well on the questions and URLS in TIFAP, but it easily outperformed the other two clients we looked at and which I later reevaluated. "Tweaked" to minimal settings, Cyber Patrol blocked "good sites" 5-10% of the time, depending on the tester, and pornographic sites slipped through about 10% of the time, which is a figure I heard also from librarians using Cyber Patrol in actual library settings.

Stories regularly pop up, and people email me, about inappropriate sites blocked by Cyber Patrol, most recently a major bookstore in San Francisco; at press time, Cyber Patrol still blocked http://www.disinfo.com, a website devoted to debunking propaganda. Cyber Patrol claims it has 85% of the filtering market; if this is the case, perhaps they could afford to hire more than 12 people to identify and categorize the Internet.

Cyber Patrol supports local site lists (access and deny), and can be enabled for RSACI or Safe Surf PICS settings in addition to Cyber Patrol settings (though see the chapter, Web Rating Systems). The PICS configuration panel is greatly improved in 4.0—I hope the rest of the program follows suit.

Local access/deny lists are easy to use from the administrative module, but still only each hold 64 URLs.

User/Workstation Configuration

Privilege Levels and Password Override

The Cyber Patrol client can support multiple users with different access levels. The "deputy bypass" setting allows immediate access to blocked resources without providing access to the administrative module.

The configuration is a bit confusing. It took several tries, and extensive coaching from one experienced user, for the TIFAP testers to configure Cyber Patrol to minimal settings. The interface in version 4.0 is slightly better, though it still needs work, and the unsettling "police station" motif has been toned down.

Resource Allocation

Cyber Patrol supports blocking by time, and in addition to blocking nntp and irc directly, has a wide variety of protocols it can block by port number (nntp, irc, ftp, gopher, telnet). However, services running on nonstandard ports could potentially be accessed if they were not blocked in some other way.

Denial Pages and User Feedback

The denial page displays a code, such as "Cyber Patrol Code 2," which will be meaningless to the end user; more to the point, this page cannot be configured to point to a library policy or link to a request form for reconsideration. The reconsideration site within the administration module is good, though if it were a form from the denial page the site in question could be captured in the message, rather than requiring the administrator to copy and paste the URL.

Performance issues

The "word on the street" from libraries that are supporting multiple client copies of Cyber Patrol (up to 50, in one system) is that it often needs reinstallation and fiddling. Cyber Patrol now supports automated downloads, though they cannot be scheduled, so this feature is only useful if you have a dedicated connection.

Administration, Reporting, Tech Support

Reporting is very limited, and does not display what is blocked or accessed. The reports do display bypasses, but it will be up to you to remember what they were. Monitoring is also unavailable. Technical support is plentiful, at least during the week, and competent.

CYBER PATROL

Company and Address
http://www.microsys.com/
info@microsys.com
Microsystems Software, Inc.
600 Worcester Road
Framingham, MA 01701
508–879–9000

Versions:
Client:
Version 4.0 was evaluated just as this book went to press.
Windows 3.1, 95, NT; Macintosh

Server:
LAN (network version of client)
Proxy plug-in for Microsoft and Netscape
Firewall
Novell Border Manager
Integration with other products on request, including products for specific firewalls

Pricing examples (Client):
$29.95 for client version; includes 3–month update. 12–month list subscription is $29.95.
Contact company for proxy, network and firewall pricing.

Technical Support:
Telephone support: 8:15–midnight, Monday through Friday
Online support on weekends as well as the week (answered within two business days)

FILTER FEATURES

Bullets • are features vendors said they would support on market demand
Italics indicate vendor-supplied information

Feature	Client	*LAN*	NS/MS
Vendor-supplied site list	Yes	*Yes*	Yes
# of staff maintaining list	*12*	12	12
View Site List	No	*No*	No
Edit Site List	No	*No*	No
Site List update frequency	Daily	*Daily*	Daily
Automated list download	Yes	*Yes*	*Yes*
Support Third-Party Lists•	No	*No*	*No*
Local access/deny lists	Yes[1]	*Yes*	*Yes*
Keyword filtering	Yes	*Yes*	*No*
Can disable keyword filtering[2]	Yes	*Yes*	*N/A*
Block to file level	Yes	*Yes*	*Yes*
Block by protocol[3]	Yes	*Yes*	*Yes*
Block by time of day	Yes	*Yes*	*Yes*
Host name resolves to IP	Yes	*Yes*	*Yes*
Support time-outs•	No	*No*	*No*
Configure by IP address•	No	*No*	*No*
Configure by user ID[4]•	No	*Yes*	*Yes*
Support patron barcodes•	No	*No*	*No*
Vendor-defined categories	Yes	*Yes*	*Yes*
Block or enable by categories	Yes	*Yes*	*Yes*
Option to warn vs. block•	No	*No*	*No*
Edit denial message•	No	*No*	Yes
PICS support	Yes	*Yes*	*Yes*
Password override	Yes	*Yes*	*Yes*
Monitor vs. block	No	*No*	*No*
Email link for reconsiderations	Yes	*Yes*	*Yes*
Multiple privilege levels	Yes	*Yes*	*Yes*
Remote administration	No	*No*	*No*
Reporting capabilities	Limited	*Limited*	*Better*

[1] Limited to 64 URLs
[2] Cannot disable "Carlin 7" keywords
[3] http blocked by all versions. LAN and client can selectively block ftp, gopher, telnet, nntp, finger; proxy server same, but by standard service port number.
[4] Using usernames and passwords

> *IN BRIEF:*
> **ONE FILTER: X-STOP**
>
> **TWO MONITORING PRODUCTS:**
> **CYBER SNOOP AND ON GUARD**

X-STOP

Log-On Data Corp.
http://www.xstop.com/
4175 East La Palma Avenue, Suite 130
Anaheim, CA 92807
1–888–786–7999
Preconfigured Server: $8896
Client: $36

X-Stop offers two products, a Windows client and a preconfigured server ("proxy-in-a-box"). X-Stop company information indicates it can block in 15 main categories, which are further subdivided into three or four subcategories, such as Entertainment—Comic Strips and Travel—Map Sites.

The product X-Stop markets to libraries is called "Felony Load," which X-Stop claims blocks only obscenity, bestiality and child pornography. One library contacted me to say X-Stop was not functioning as advertised. I tried for six months, without success, to evaluate the proxy-server version of the product. A volunteer finally procured access to the X-Stop client just before this book went to press. This filter blocked Planned Parenthood, a safe-sex Website, several gay advocacy sites, and sites with information that would rate as highly risque, but not obscene, let alone felonious.

In a post to the FILT4LIB discussion group, Karen Gounaud of Family Friendly Libraries claimed the X-Stop company had "achieved 100% success." She went on to say,

> They don't even require a sea of people to be employed just to watch porn all day. It's automated through a combination of mathematics, probability, common sense . . .

Caveat emptor. No product is 100% effective, and other products do rely on "a sea of people" for their comparably-priced filters. X-Stop has been endorsed by such organizations as Family Friendly Libraries, the Family Research Council, Enough Is Enough, and the American Family Association.

TWO MONITORING PRODUCTS

Cyber Snoop
http://www.pearlsw.com/
Pearl Software, Inc.
P.O. Box 387
Chester Springs, PA 19403
1–(800)-PEARL96
sales@pearlsw.com

On Guard
http://www.on.com/ogim/
ON Technology Corporation,
One Cambridge Ctr
Cambridge, MA 02142
TEL (617) 374–1400, FAX (617) 374–1433
info@on.com

Both Cyber Snoop and On Guard market their filtering capabilities, but Cyber Snoop comes with an inadequate list and On Guard comes with none. Forget their tentative foray into the filtering market and focus on their monitoring capabilities. The only thing you will miss that filter products offer is the reporting by category, but if you are alert to URL naming conventions and other tricks, you should at least get a good sense of what's happening.

Three TIFAP people installed and looked at Cyber Snoop. For $30 per workstation, you could do a lot worse; it beats spending close to ten thousand dollars to address a problem you don't have. Cyber Snoop installs simply and well, and reports by date, protocol or even keyword. Technical support is prompt and courteous. The help section is a bit brief; I would have liked more discussion about its log-sorting capabilities, for example. I wish that Cyber Snoop broke down its reports by categories, but a Web-savvy librarian should be able to divine some of the pornography sites, since these often have names suggestive of what they are describing.

One TIFAP tester installed On Guard and ran it through its paces. At $2650 for a 50–user license—the entry-level purchase for this product—On Guard isn't cheap. On the other hand, it looks like a fabulous toy—I mean tool—for network administrators. Click a button to display sites, workstations and groups of workstations; another click brings you to a dialog for reports and graphs, which can be further refined by a date/time feature. The documentation is extensive; just the section on "Starting and Stopping" On Guard took two very thorough pages, with seven graphics. Reporting is flexible and detailed.

APPENDICES

3j.   What is the nicotine content of different brands of cigarettes?

3k.   What drug is a bong used for?

3l.   What are the symptoms of an Ecstasy overdose?

4.   Gay issues

4a.   I want information on PFLAG.

4b.   What did Virginia Ramey Mollenkott write?

4c.   Can you find me more information about Leslea Newman, author of *Heather Has Two Mommies*?

4d.   I'm looking for the press releases surrounding Ellen DeGeneres.

4e.   I have a friend at school who told me he thinks he's gay. Are there discussion groups for gay teens I can tell him about?

4f.   I need some information and a picture of the Enola Gay.

4g.   In what poem did Robert Frost write, "my little horse must think it queer"?

4h.   I live in Kansas and I want to build an igloo. Can you find directions on-line for building an igloo?

4i.   Can you find some information about the case of the radio announcer who was fired for reading Ginsberg's "Howl" on the air?

4j.   Was the author of *Alice in Wonderland* gay? How about Gertrude Stein?

4k.   What are the latest AIDS medications being prescribed?

4l.   Can you get AIDS from fisting?

5.   Crimes (including pedophilia and child pornography)

5a.   What was the name of the guy in Ohio who was convicted for kidnapping, molesting and cutting up young men?

5b.   Does Charles Manson have an email address?

5c.   I'm a farmer and I want to research rape—the plant used to make canola oil.

5d.   I want information on how to take photographs of children.

5e.   I want information on the National Man-Boy Love Association.

5f.   I want information about the charges against Jeff Smith (the Frugal Gourmet) concerning child molestation accusations

Appendix A:
Questions for Evaluating
Filter Performance

These questions were available in a password-protected directory to TIFAP volunteers. Some of the questions are double entendres intended to trip up keyword-blocking mechanisms; others were designed to test how filters perform on controversial content. See the chapter about The Internet Filter Assessment Project for how these questions were used. If you are evaluating a filter, you can use these questions to evaluate how well the filter performs.

Categories

1. Sex and pornography
2. Anatomy
3. Drugs, alcohol and tobacco
4. Gay issues
5. Crimes (including pedophilia and child pornography)
6. Obscene or "racy" language
7. Culture and religion
8. Women's issues
9. Gambling
10. Hate groups and intolerance
11. Politics

Questions

1.   Sex and pornography

1a.   I'd like some information on safe sex.

1b.   I'd like to find out what I can do to protect children from pornography on the web, including hard-core pornography and child pornography.

1c.   I want to know if masturbation is bad for you.

1d.   Can you find me some pictures from *Babes in Toyland*?

1e.   Is there anything on the web about the play "Playboy of the Western World"?

1f.   Is there any information on anti-pornography groups?

1g.   I want to do some research on Robert Mapplethorpe.

1h.   What's the profitability of X-rated movies?

1i.   I need pictures of antique sextants for a research paper I'm doing on sailing ships throughout history.

1j.   I'm almost 90 years old, in great physical shape, but I've suddenly developed problems maintaining erections. Is this common? What can I do about it? Would a penile implant help?

1k.   I operate a small stable. I need information on harness making.

1l.   Can I get information about Super Bowl XXX?

1m.   What are the best methods for finding wall studs for home remodeling projects?

1n.   I need some reading-level-appropriate sex education material for my six-year-old.

1o.   I'm a parapalegic. I've met a wonderful woman and we plan to marry. We need some information on sex for physically challenged people.

1p.   I'm looking for the history of syphilis—treatment, legends, folklore, etc.

1q.   How do beavers make their dams?

1r.   Besides earmuffs, what other kinds of muffs are there?

1s.   I'm looking for the website for Roger Hedgecock.

1t.   Do you have a recipe for banana cream pie?

2. Anatomy

2a.   I'd like to see Marcel DuChamp's "Nude Descending a Staircase."

2b.   I need some recipes for using up chicken breasts.

2c.   My son says he can type the phrase "naked women" in a browser and he'll see dirty pictures. Is this true?

2d.   Theo Colburn, in *Our Stolen Future*, discusses estrogenic disruptors and their impact on aquatic animals, specifically alligators with unusually small penises. What other information can you find on this topic?

2e.   I have just been diagnosed with breast cancer. What does that mean?

2f.   What are some common diseases associated with the vagina?

2g.   I'm doing a paper on cruelty to animals, including bullfighting and cockfighting.

2h.   I need a review of *The Naked Civil Servant*.

2i.   What is the full text of the nursery rhyme, "Pussy Cat, Pussy Cat"?

2j.   Where can I find information on menstruation for my daughter?

2k.   What is the latest information on companies who supplied the material for breast implants? Is there a class action suit still alive?

3. Drugs, alcohol and tobacco

3a.   Can I find a website for Joe Camel?

3b.   I'm looking for web headshops that sell paraphernalia for smoking marijuana.

3c.   I want information on the legalization of marijuana.

3d.   How is cocaine made?

3e.   Does marijuana really enhance sex?

3f.   What is the exact text of the California medical use of marijuana law?

3g.   What are some of the common household substances that kids are abusing?

3h.   Do you have the information from the first Clinton campaign where he talked about "not inhaling"?

3i.   I need a recipe for Long Island Tea (alcoholic).

3j.   What is the nicotine content of different brands of cigarettes?

3k.   What drug is a bong used for?

3l.   What are the symptoms of an Ecstasy overdose?

4. Gay issues

4a.   I want information on PFLAG.

4b.   What did Virginia Ramey Mollenkott write?

4c.   Can you find me more information about Leslea Newman, author of *Heather Has Two Mommies*?

4d.   I'm looking for the press releases surrounding Ellen DeGeneres.

4e.   I have a friend at school who told me he thinks he's gay. Are there discussion groups for gay teens I can tell him about?

4f.   I need some information and a picture of the Enola Gay.

4g.   In what poem did Robert Frost write, "my little horse must think it queer"?

4h.   I live in Kansas and I want to build an igloo. Can you find directions on-line for building an igloo?

4i.   Can you find some information about the case of the radio announcer who was fired for reading Ginsberg's "Howl" on the air?

4j.   Was the author of *Alice in Wonderland* gay? How about Gertrude Stein?

4k.   What are the latest AIDS medications being prescribed?

4l.   Can you get AIDS from fisting?

5. Crimes (including pedophilia and child pornography)

5a.   What was the name of the guy in Ohio who was convicted for kidnapping, molesting and cutting up young men?

5b.   Does Charles Manson have an email address?

5c.   I'm a farmer and I want to research rape—the plant used to make canola oil.

5d.   I want information on how to take photographs of children.

5e.   I want information on the National Man-Boy Love Association.

5f.   I want information about the charges against Jeff Smith (the Frugal Gourmet) concerning child molestation accusations

5g.   What was all that fuss about PeeWee Herman a couple years ago? Was he convicted?

5h.   I want to learn how to make a fertilizer bomb like the one in Oklahoma City.

5i.   What's the definition of "mayhem"?

5j.   I'm trying to find out about the Paul Newman movie *The Hustler*.

5k.   What is the law about released pedophiles? Are neighborhoods in my state notified on their release?

5l.   In Maryland a Nobel prize-winner was just convicted of molesting boys. How can I find out about his background?

6.   Obscene or "racy" language

6a.   What were George Carlin's naughty words?

6b.   Who said "Damn the torpedos, full speed ahead"?

6c.   My dachsund is a breeder bitch. How old should she be before I breed her for the first time?

6d.   I'd like information on "fighting cock" cigars.

6e.   I want to do some research on screw threads, screws, and screwing down machinery.

6f.   What is the derivation of the term "mud people"? What groups make common use of this term and what can I find out about them?

6g.   What is the definition of the Yiddish term, "momzer"?

6h.   I need information about Hooters, the restaurant chain.

7.   Culture and Religion

7a.   Do any of the mail order bride companies have a web page?

7b.   Are there any local Wicca groups in the area? How do they celebrate the summer solstice?

7c.   Is there a pagan church in my neighborhood?
       What Coptic sacraments involve marijuana?

7d.   Religious use of peyote was recently approved by the US military. Where can I find more information?

7e.   I'm looking for information on Santoria and voodoo.

7f.   What has happened to Madelyn Murray O'Hare?

7g.   I'm writing a paper on Harvey Milk. I need information about Jimmy Jones and the Peoples Temple movement.

7h.   I'm an adherent of the Wiccan faith. Are there any covens in my region of the country?

8.   Women's Issues

8a.   Where can I get some information on the use of different forms of birth control used by women around the world?

8b.   I need the email address for the National Organization of Women.

8c.   I need information on abortion from both sides of the issue, pro-life and pro-choice.

8d.   What was the name of the young woman who petitioned the US government to give her asylum because she was fleeing cliterodectomy in her native country?

8e.   I'm looking for a discussion group on breastfeeding.

8f.   I'm pregnant and I have herpes.

9.   Gambling

9a.   I'm can't remember his name, but I'm looking for a jockey who raced at the Santa Anita racetrack sometime in the last month. I'll know his name if I see it.

9b.   What's the best way to win at casino games?

10.   Hate groups and intolerance

10a.   For a paper on weather systems, I need information about stormfronts.

10b.   Do you have the email address and website for the John Birch Society?

10c.   My uncle told me last night he belongs to the Ku Klux Klan. I'm worried about him. Can you find a website for the Klan so I can see what they do and believe?

10d.   Is the Aryan Nation the same thing as Nazis?

10e.   HateWatch is the premier organization for tracking a variety of hate groups outreach efforts on the web. Can I access their website?

11. Politics

11a. Who are the founders of the Electronic Frontier Foundation and what does it stand for?

11b. What is PGP? Why is there a legal controversy about it? Who invented it?

11c. I've heard that the National Security Agency wants to mandate the use of the Clipper chip in telecommunications, where can I find more information?

11d. How do I find the Militia of Montana or the truth about Ruby Ridge?

11e. Did the CIA really assassinate JFK, RFK, and MLK?

11f. What state has the most prisoners on Death Row? Which state has executed the most prisoners since the reinstatement of the death penalty?

11g. Why did the FBI raid Steve Jackson Games (SJG)?

Appendix B:
Ten Useful URLs

A Practical Guide to Internet Filters
http://www.bluehighways.com/filters/
The website for this book, where you will find additional information related to filters.

The Internet Filter Assessment Project
http://www.bluehighways.com/tifap/
The website for TIFAP, the project that launched this book. (Also linked from the book website.)

Voters Telecommunication Watch
http://www.vtw.org
A good-government site; I'm donating 10% of my royalties from my book to VTW to help establish a newsletter on intellectual freedom.

Cyber Kids
http://metronet.lib.mi.us/CANT/youth.html
An Internet program for children at Canton Public Library, Michigan, discussed in Chapter 6, "Advice from the Trenches." A good model to study.

"Internet Freedom and Filters"

http://www.csn.net/~jlarue/iff.html

James LaRue's extremely thoughtful, balanced discussion of the problems facing us today. Includes practical suggestions, links to Internet policies, and historical background.

LibraryLand—The Intellectual Freedom Section

http://www.rcls.org/libland/cen/cens.htm

Jerry Kuntz conducted two sets of filter-vendor surveys this year. Libraryland—overall an excellent resource in its own right—has an excellent section on resources related to Internet filters, including links to his vendor surveys.

Library Policy Website

http://www.ci.oswego.or.us/library/poli.htm

David Burt's Library Policy Website, which includes many good examples of library policies

Matrix Information and Directory Services

http://www.mids.org

John S. Quarterman offers some free data related to the measurement of Internet services, but also sells several high-quality serials on this topic.

Network Wizards

http://wwww.nw.com

This is another good site for Internet statistics. (They asked to be cited if I used their statistics, which I do in the introduction to this book.)

Child Safety on the Information Superhighway

http://www.missingkids.org

This website provides free pamphlets to educate parents about the potential hazards related to children and the Internet.